A

Finding belief and possibility in life's impossible moments

FRAC-
TION
STRO-
NGER

Mark Berridge

MAJOR
STREET

Praise for *A Fraction Stronger*

Don't just buy one copy of this book – buy a copy for your partner, your family members, your workmates and anyone who has ever given you a leg-up in life. *A Fraction Stronger* reminds you that hope is a choice. It will help you find the freedom you need to live without fear, to love with courage and to triumph in the face of adversity. Above all, it will inspire you to always choose the life you have, and to live it with passion.
Anne Savage, CEO, Prostate Cancer Foundation of Australia

This book is inspirational, no doubt about it, but before it gets there it is a brutally honest exploration of the self-doubt, guilt, pain, setbacks and emotional roller-coaster that impacts everyone at some point or another, especially those impacted by serious injury. *A Fraction Stronger* is a beautifully written story about Mark's journey back from a horrific accident and the power of determination, resilience, perseverance, courage and the help and support we all need when the chips are down. I defy anyone to read this book and not be a better person for the experience.
Brad Shaw, CEO, InterFinancial Corporate Finance Limited

A book I will read again and again. In sharing his personal learnings and the stories of others, Mark provides a raw, real and practical guide to help you achieve what your mind first sees as impossible. I wish I'd had this book by my side when smashing glass ceilings in male-dominated industries and when I was told my young daughter had leukaemia, because it is full of powerful, personal reflections to get your mind focusing forward, a fraction at a time.
Sharon Warburton, Non-executive Director – Wesfarmers Limited, WA Telstra Business Woman of the Year, and cancer mum

A Fraction Stronger is an emotional, engaging and valuable read. Mark is so vulnerable and open about his experience you can't help being there with him, sharing in his challenges and successes. Full of powerful yet practical ideas for any individual to face the 'impossible moments' in their own life, this story of Mark's remarkable journey left me feeling 'a fraction stronger'.
John Malitoris, President, Malitoris Associates

Mark has never looked for a short cut or a fad, or opted for the easy path. His willingness to consistently chase those 1 per cent improvements is what makes him a champion. Through his grit and determination, he has redefined what is possible.
Miranda O'Hara, M. Musculoskeletal & Sports Phty, MPhty, BEd (HMHE), Founder and Owner – Restore Function Physiotherapy

A Fraction Stronger is an exceptional and poignant personal journey of courage told with poetic humility. Mark gives voice to the importance of not only recognising one's vulnerabilities but rediscovering the capacity to visualise what's possible, of finding light and hope despite the seductive and corrosive demons of self-doubt.

Readers have been provided a gift that will encourage them to open courageous conversations when confronted with the unexpected challenges that demand that they find a way to become *A Fraction Stronger*.

Mark Spatz, Partner, Negotiation Partners

Life has a habit of throwing up challenges when we are least prepared for them. Be they physical, deeply emotional, or even fiscal, it is *how* we respond and grow through these challenges that really matters. Sadly, it is the 'how' that so often remains elusive. In *A Fraction Stronger* Mark shares his own story of challenge and commitment to ongoing recovery. Demonstrating extraordinary resilience, he delivers up the 'how' through practical wisdom and guidance that could see all of us through testing times.

Ann-Maree David, Executive Director (Queensland), The College of Law

This is a courageous story of how life can change in a split second, how new perspectives on success are formed, and the mental power and strength to start the daunting road back. When sport and a healthy life always shaped and defined you, and these are taken away in a moment, a new life and a long road to recovery begins. There is much inspiration and many life lessons in this powerful, emotional and impactful book. Well done Mark on being brave and having the determination to come back, and to share your story.

Andrew Wildblood, Chief Executive, Enterprise and Government, Vocus

Mark's book offers valuable keys to overcome issues, set goals and project oneself from a very difficult situation. It is applicable to many situations even without going through a traumatic injury or life-changing experience. Drawing from different stages of life, from his own situation and other inspirational stories, from personal and professional life experiences, the book made me relate to situations we face every day and how to overcome them. But beyond all else, it is a powerful reminder of how to support others through difficult events.

Amélie Hennion, Managing Director, ALVANCE Aluminium Group

Many of us have had to overcome some major challenges in our lives. When you read about Mark's challenges arising from a simple biking accident, it is likely that your own experiences will pale into insignificance. Mark writes his story to be less about his fall and more about how he chose to get up. He offers lots of practical tips, both mental and physical, about his recovery. I particularly commend his story to anyone who is seeking pathways to recover from a major fall in life.

Phillip Strachan, Non-executive Board Chair/Director

This book is a treasure trove of gold nuggets that will either challenge, comfort or inspire you! Mark tells his story so that you never have to feel alone, which is why you'll want to read it again and again.
Dr Ruth Knight, Postdoctoral Research Fellow, The Australian Centre for Philanthropy and Nonprofit Studies, QUT

Mark Berridge was my hockey captain in Hong Kong. Aside from concentrating on their own game, captains monitor, lead and support the team. Mark excels in this role, with his consistent positive attitude to sport and life generally. When your leader is constantly positive, encouraging and happy it becomes infectious. Mark guided us through significant challenges, achieving results way beyond expectations. That same positive attitude guided Mark through his recovery and is the foundation for his book.
Angus Emmerson, APAC Legal Counsel, *Financial Times*

An open, honest and motivating story that will increase your empathy and understanding of recovery after trauma, plus motivational tips to lead your best life. Mark's storytelling allows you to gain life skills in how to support someone emotionally through recovery. This book weaves the long road of Mark's recovery with inspirational courage and anecdotes from other people's experiences. It is confronting at times but ultimately uplifting as Mark challenges you, the reader, to explore hope, possibility and surrounding yourself with people that support open-minded thinking.
'Never die wondering.'
Helen Galloway, Non-executive Director: Bank of us, Hydro Tasmania, TT-Line, Tasracing

A Fraction Stronger is much more than just a practical strategic blueprint for incremental recovery from traumatic physical catastrophe. It offers insightful and inspirational ideas for overcoming many difficulties in our daily lives. I have already incorporated some of Mark's thoughtful recommendations into my daily activities. Mark Berridge has revealed the inner workings of his soul to the reader and in that process has shared his wisdom with the world.
Recommended!
Paul Isaac, IT Manager, Mullins Lawyers

First published in 2022 by Major Street Publishing Pty Ltd
info@majorstreet.com.au | +61 421 707 983 | majorstreet.com.au

A catalogue record for this book is available
from the National Library of Australia

Printed book ISBN: 978-1-922611-28-4
Ebook ISBN: 978-1-922611-29-1

Cover design by Tess McCabe
Author photograph by Rebecca Taylor Photography
Internal design by Production Works
Printed in Australia by IVE Group, an Accredited ISO AS/NZS 14001:2004
Environmental Management System Printer.

10 9 8 7 6 5 4 3 2 1

Contents

Preface   ix
Introduction   1

PART I: LANTERNS   **11**

Chapter 1   Finding your brave face   15
Chapter 2   Embracing uncertainty   25
Chapter 3   Liberating possibility   39
Chapter 4   Raking your embers   49
Chapter 5   Exploring pathways   63

PART II: ANGELS   **79**

Chapter 6   Reaching out and in   83
Chapter 7   Applying effort   94
Chapter 8   Fostering belief   108
Chapter 9   Uniting through love   121

PART III: DEMONS   **131**

Chapter 10   Reframing guilt   135
Chapter 11   Facing fear   148
Chapter 12   Dealing with despair   160
Chapter 13   Finding worth   172

Now a fraction stronger   185
Gratitude   193
About the author   195
References   197

*I pay my respect to the Aboriginal and Torres Strait Islander
ancestors of this land, their spirits and their legacy.*

*I acknowledge and pay respect to the traditional
elders of our nation: past, present and future.*

*The foundations laid by these ancestors give strength,
inspiration and courage to current and future generations,
both Indigenous and non-Indigenous.*

*I hope our nation can unite to foster a deep, ongoing
custodianship of this sacred country – its land, rivers and sea –
as its traditional owners always aspired to do.*

*I thank the spirit of Biami Yumba Park for helping me
get up from my fall, with the strength and self-development
initiated there on 10 March 2019.*

Preface

My first five years were spent in the Western Australian (WA) beachside town of Geraldton. I suspect it was where my dad was happiest, harvesting crays, herring and tailor from the ocean in our little tinny. Mum would take us to the beach often and I particularly relished it. I still love the ocean.

We had a boofy blond Labrador named Guy, and he was my first beachside guardian. Mum credits him for saving me many a time, as I crawled my way into the ocean before she could so much as put down a beach towel or prop up our heavy canvas beach umbrella. Guy would see me charging into the little waves and grab my swimmers in his mouth, just as I got out of my depth, dragging me back a few metres towards the shore.

In the summer of 1982–83, we moved back to Geraldton for a second time. I was 11. My parents decided my older brother, Peter, and I could invite a friend each up from Roleystone to join us in our new beachside life. The four of us spent our week together, canoeing the local Chapman River, playing cricket and table tennis and enjoying the nearby beach.

I loved exploring sand dunes, perhaps as a result of our regular holidays at Hamelin Bay in the south-west of WA. Hence, I was probably the instigator as the four of us hared our way through the sand dunes at the northern side of Sunset Beach one scorching hot day. We walked out beyond the nudist beach to where there was nothing. Just scorching sun, perfectly white sand and the vast ocean. The only sounds were the crashing of waves.

The sand was so hot we had to keep our feet wet by staying on the damp sand where the whitewash ebbed and flowed. We played tag and brandy with a wet tennis ball and dipped in the shallows, always on the edge of the strong surf.

And then, as younger boys can, we triggered anger. It is not a unique skill among siblings, but I was particularly talented at antagonising Peter.

My friend Johnny and I could not outrun the older boys, so next thing we knew we were running deeper into the ocean, getting out of our depth. The waves were large, and we were in trouble. In an instant we were caught in their dumping path, getting sucked under and then out to sea by the force of the ocean. Perhaps it took two or three big waves before the older boys realised the extent of our danger, how we were struggling for air between breaking waves and unable to regain our footing or swim in against the strong backwash.

The next time I surfaced I could see Peter's friend, Bradley, coming out towards us, reaching the edge of where he could safely stand, one line of breaking waves closer to the beach than our perilous position. And he began yelling. Encouraging us. I was exhausted from the constant dumping of the waves and the struggle against their surge, but his voice compelled me to make more effort, and he helped me focus those efforts.

He coached us about what waves were coming and what to do, meaning we could look forward to the shore and not waste energy looking back to the danger. His guidance stopped us from getting caught turning into the breaking waves at the wrong moments, as we had been doing. He helped us get dumped less often, which reduced the amount we were being dragged out to sea by each returning wave. He coached us into stronger positions to get sufficient momentum from the breaking waves so we could edge back towards the beach.

Bradley supported and encouraged us until we found our feet, until we were securely on the shore, exhausted but relieved. I have always believed he saved me that day, just like Guy the Labrador had all those years before.

In March 2019, the crushing impact of a bicycle accident stranded me in a dry stormwater drain. In the moments, days and months that followed, I regularly felt like I was back among those crashing waves. Out of my depth, feeling exhausted, losing hope. But this time I had a team of Guys and Bradleys standing on the beach, coaching me back towards safety.

With their incredible help, I faced some tough moments to reach better outcomes. Again.

Physically I might not quite get back to the shore this time – walking on flat land now requires the same energy as if I were pushing through shallow water. I have learned to cope with altered balance and foot sensation, in a similar way to how your feet feel different as you negotiate through those shallows. And I will always be knee deep in a bit of turbulence – the fatigue, the niggles, the physical deficiencies. Periods of smoother passage, and surges of rougher water.

Physically everything in life is just harder. I am still focused on improving, and I won't ever give up the hope of adding further improvements as I close in on my best possible physical outcome.

My physicality is only one of the outcomes as I beat the break this time. I am a different and stronger person. I found resilience in difficulty.

My journey forged many great friendships – souls united through love and care. It generated fabulous memories out of the challenges tackled and overcome, out of the failures and the comical mishaps that happen in life, in any hard journey. Lessons that reinforce my belief in what I can achieve. Embers that make me glow.

The accident caused me to reconnect with elements of my identity that I loved as a child. To be creative. To write. This was a part of me that had been neglected for much of my career while I chased meaning from my expanding roles and responsibilities as I climbed that corporate ladder.

The events of 10 March 2019 changed the trajectory of my life. They enabled me to become a fraction stronger (again) and provided the stimulus to share these words. My good fortune to get up, and grasp the opportunity to try with all my resolve, has generated a story that I hope might support others in finding their possibilities. For that I am immensely grateful.

Introduction

The day my life changed forever started out much like a typical Sunday. I reached for my iPad in the pre–5 a.m. darkness to shut off the soft intro chords of Ed Sheeran's 'The A Team' before it disturbed my wife, Lucy. For a moment, I considered staying in bed. The previous days had been long and tiring, as I had worked with colleagues to put the finishing touches on the workshop we were to deliver in Salt Lake City the coming week. But I knew early morning exercise would help me sleep during that evening's long-haul flight to the US, so I willed myself out of bed and into the quiet morning, leaving Lucy and our three teenage kids to their peaceful slumber.

Within minutes I was pedalling my bike through the silent Coorparoo streets towards my cycling crew's rendezvous point, feeling good about my decision to push through the fatigue. I knew I'd lose cycling fitness while I was in the US, and getting this one last ride in could fractionally reduce that impact. I always focused on grasping marginal gains. But it was much more than just exercise – I valued the camaraderie of the group. We called ourselves the COGs – Coorparoo Older Guys – because mostly we were acquainted through the local schools our children attended in or around that Brisbane suburb. We were united in our shared love of cycling, but it went deeper than that, with many important friendships establishing as we rode.

I'd joined the group a couple of years before as I strived to improve my health and fitness. The cycling captain, Stewart (Stewy), had been one of the first people I'd met when I moved to Brisbane 20 years earlier. Stewy and I had formed an important bond, staying in close contact as our children grew up together, our families intertwining as we became godparents to each other's children.

It took a tough, sustained effort to bring myself up towards the fitness standard set by the COGs. I could readily have given up on many of the early rides, feeling defeated and embarrassed as I regularly fell away from the pack. But I persevered, and in the moments of choosing to do so, I had no idea the COGs and our rides would become such a treasured part of my life. We did 40 km 'river loops' two or three times each week, plus the Sunday ritual of a longer ride – typically around 70 km, but sometimes up to 110 km.

As we rode that Sunday morning, I chatted proudly as I relived the prior day's cricket action at Villanova College – my sons' school. My eldest son, Luke, had taken an important catch and saved many runs in the field as his side prevailed in a seesawing game against their strongest rival. This offset my youngest son's disappointment as his team was thumped by the same school. Charlie, a natural leader, never stopped trying to lift his team and took a key wicket.

Between periods of chatting, I cherished the harmony of cycling with the crew. I had discovered my love of cycling many years before, riding to and from my first full-time job. I started riding to avoid the frustration of erratic bus timetables and soon found that cycling provided me the headspace for thought and reflection, plus the satisfying release of extending myself with intense periods of physical effort. I enjoyed challenging myself to pedal as hard as I could, hurtling my second-hand mountain bike along the Swan River foreshore in Perth, competing with those on much faster bikes.

As we rode that morning, I reflected on the past few weeks of intense preparation for the Salt Lake City workshop. I was proud of our work, confident our initiatives would secure the longer-term future for our client and its 200-plus workers. I allowed myself to daydream about the sneaky skiing weekend I planned to squeeze into the trip, remembering the near-perfect conditions we'd enjoyed on Salt Lake City's slopes during our previous visit. They were two of the best ski days ever – at Alta with three of the team on Saturday and skiing Solitude alone on the Sunday.

As I coasted down Fig Tree Pocket Road alongside my crew, I remember thinking, 'How beautiful is the weather this morning? How perfect to be able to cycle like this.'

Then, in a fraction of a moment, my whole world changed.

I could see the corner ahead and watched the six other riders as they slowed around it, using that information to plan my turn. Pip, Dave and I were a bit behind the pack, riding single file, giving us the chance to corner a fraction quicker. Braking to a safe speed, I felt balanced, enjoying that magical feeling of cornering my bike. Then suddenly my front wheel wasn't gripping the road. Rather than pedalling through and out of the corner as planned, I was skating straight ahead, momentarily out of control.

In a split second I processed my options and decided to crash into the grassy parkland ahead, even though I could see both a 90-degree kerb and pine barriers, which meant I'd be flung over the handlebars for sure.

I remember the terrible sensation of my shoes being wrenched from their cleats and my hands being ripped from their grip on my brake levers as my body weight surged forward, catapulted from my bike.

I felt my head striking the ground – hard – followed by my body slamming down on its side. Then the intense, searing pain hit me. Gasping, I realised I couldn't breathe properly: my pain, shock and injuries combined to cause short, shallow pants.

I could feel the sensation of dirt under my left side, but I couldn't move or look around. Suddenly I felt someone near me – Dave. I could hear Mike talking in the distance, on the phone getting emergency assistance.

'The ambulance is on its way, Berro', he said.

My impactful moments

In the early hours of 10 March 2019, the trajectory of my life changed forever. In a fraction of a moment, I went from cruising downhill enjoying the freshness of the morning air and beautiful sunshine, to hitting a sunken, slippery piece of bitumen repair work, causing my bicycle to understeer through its cornering line. Bereft of viable options, I chose what I felt was the best of my bad alternatives: braking and crashing straight ahead into a park. It is incredible how quickly you seem to be able to process information, and the detail you recall of those thoughts that took just fractions of seconds.

My bike bounced up the kerb and slammed into the park's pine bollard boundary. I flew high from my bike and came down in a stormwater drain, about 1.5 metres below the road level. My left hand probably hit the bluestone rock wall edge of the drain first. My trajectory drove my head into that same rock and my left shoulder hard into the ground. The impact crushed the left side of my helmet.

Around four hours after my accident, I learned the shocking extent of the damage. The force that went through my helmet as I struck the ground had compressed two of my vertebrae, crushing one to just 40 per cent of its original height. A large fragment of that vertebra had burst into my spinal cord, causing nerve damage and compressing the space available for the spinal cord to function. I had also fractured my left shoulder and wrist, and three ribs.

At the exact hour I was due to depart Brisbane for Salt Lake City, I was in the operating theatre with a team of experts inserting two 23 cm rods into my back to stabilise my spine. I didn't know it yet, but that work trip was the first of many aspects of my life that would be displaced by my misadventure – my immediate career, my ability to walk, my role in the family.

Fortunately, many crucial aspects of my life were spared by the quality of my recently acquired helmet. I'd been eyeing off new bikes when I stumbled on that $300 helmet, marked down to $150 in the New Year sales. Fate was looking after me that day. The helmet protected my ability to comprehend, to think and to recall valuable memories. These have provided – and will continue to provide – the comfort of the past, perspectives on the present and inspiration for the future. And it is this that affords me this privilege of describing my story and recovery – to relate to you the experiences and learnings that supported my journey and how these can be powerful for you, too, no matter your circumstances in life.

A fraction stronger

As I write this book, more than two years after the accident, I am still a work in progress – as I will be for my remaining life. I am slower. I need to be careful with my balance. Every action takes a lot more energy and getting off the floor is difficult. But I have been able to recapture much of my mobility, and I am grateful for that.

The disruption to my sense of identity was the most unsettling aspect. In a split second the immediate pathway of my life became vastly different – as if my crushed vertebrae represented the next two stepping-stones of my life, and these had just shattered before me. Instead of co-leading a workshop in the US, I would be doing my best to picture my meaningful future from a bed in acute care.

I had many disrupted thoughts: who am I now? What parts of my former self can I get back? How do I do that? What are my true colours? What values will I stand for?

5

I was doing everything I could to stay positive, to look forward. But it was a wrestle.

I was feeling sorry for myself. I was expending energy reflecting on the accident and what went wrong. I was lonely and fearful of setbacks. I was overwhelmed with guilt that I was going to be a burden to my family. I was weighed down with doubt.

Energy is precious. Dwelling on things beyond your control will exhaust you. I realised that I needed to limit the thoughts that distracted me from my recovery. I had to concentrate my attention on the actions that would move me towards my vision of recovery from the current moment.

I had to become a fraction stronger, then a fraction stronger again – repeatedly.

I had to work hard to release myself from the burden of doubt. I gave myself permission to tolerate uncertainty – because only by embracing uncertainty can we liberate possibility. Only by letting go of the distractions can we obtain the clarity and focus we need to make sure our effort supports our goals.

You won't get it right every moment, every day. I certainly didn't. But you can make it a habit you revert to, to keep you on that pathway to your vision.

By navigating our tough moments, we discover who we are. We build connections that support us for life. We rebuild that sense of identity that is slipping away. I have been there. I came back stronger. Different, but stronger. And no matter what you're facing right now – whether it's a physical or emotional challenge – you can, too.

Lanterns, angels and demons

From my first fragile days in hospital, I felt enormous gratitude. For the paramedics who got me to the hospital safely, the nurses who cared for me, the quality of my surgery and the kindness of strangers and acquaintances. And most of all, the love of family and friends.

As I navigated my rehabilitation journey, I could see the contrast between my conviction and positivity in the face of challenges and some of the patients around me. I would often receive comments like 'The physios must love you' from people familiar with the recovery process. It seemed that my commitment to improve was quite unusual, which surprised me. I welcomed any assistance I received during my recovery, and I thrived under the care of those helping me.

My experience instilled in me a deep desire to 'give back' – to help others like me wade through the challenges of dealing with change and trauma. During 2020 I wrote a few short articles encouraging others to find their way towards better outcomes, conveying how important the support that I received had been for me. I received positive feedback on how my articles had helped people, and I found the writing was helping me, too. I was starting to address the demons that I still hadn't conquered – to deal with my guilt, the transitions I was still working my way through. My lament for lost physical capabilities, the uncertainty about how I might regain my family and career identities.

The three parts of this book are based around the streams of thinking that were integral to my physical recovery, and in that transition to a rebuilt identity:

1. What is the most exceptional outcome I might achieve from here?
2. What will drive me towards that exceptional outcome?
3. What feelings do I have about where I am and the journey ahead? How do I use them positively, as motivation to persevere?

I call these lanterns, angels and demons. Lanterns help us see possibility; angels help us move forward; and demons could derail us, unless we reframe them as motivation.

If just a few more people can become a fraction stronger traversing their journey with the help of my insights – and if this strength drives them to achieve better outcomes – that is an incredibly valuable thing. Valuable to the individual, to their family, their friends, and to those thousands of people just doing their job: being kind, sharing expertise, helping random people like me recover, day after day. More efforts to applaud, more successes to celebrate. More joy.

I wrote this book because I want more people to strive for and obtain their own positive feedback, their own feeling of grace and fortitude. Because that was so valuable to me.

Your exceptional outcome

This book will help you to navigate a difficult disruption – whatever that means in your life. It will help you take action; to believe you can make it through. 2020 and 2021 were difficult years for so many people, with COVID-19 impacting routines, families and careers, and curtailing so many precious lives before their time. The pandemic was the catalyst for me to start writing about my own journey, as I realised that people face and overcome disruption all the time – my own challenges were, in so many ways, not unique. We are all doing our best to find our way in this often complex and difficult world. And that perseverance through difficulty is valuable, because life on the other side can provide us so much delight and joy.

I am convinced my recovery was powered by my ability to visualise my exceptional outcome; my determination to foster and strengthen that vision, and to fight for it when it was becoming distant; and my capacity to reframe my demons into sources of motivation, helping me persevere towards that vision.

What do I mean by 'exceptional outcome'? To me, an exceptional outcome is a stretch target. It's something that is difficult to achieve – perhaps next to impossible. Something that requires sustained belief, effort and focus to pursue. To pursue the exceptional, your fulfilment should be as much about the attitude and actions as the outcome itself, because most likely that stretch target will be just beyond grasp. Be guided by the great Renaissance artist Michelangelo, who is believed to have said, 'The greatest danger for most of us is not that our aim is too high and we miss it, but that it is too low and we reach it'.

I had to find a way to keep my exceptional outcome front of mind at my lowest points – when I was devastated by shock, fearful of my future and feeling guilty about the impact I was having on my family. Perhaps you feel some of those powerful emotions now.

The achievements of people around me, people I had met or heard of, were central to my ability to visualise my best possible outcome, to generate hope, to try. The belief I gained from the effort and achievements of others was vital, and I want this book to provide you with the belief that you can do it too. The stories I've shared about other people's journeys in this book were those that inspired me during my recovery. Some of these were influential right after my accident; some became important as I progressed. Others are simply powerful and worth sharing. All of the stories I share are about everyday people responding to adversity in a multitude of inspiring ways.

The book is designed so you can focus on a particular interest or need. It does not need to be read from cover to cover. Focusing on small sections will be beneficial, especially if reading absorbs too much energy to be sustained – as it did for me in those first weeks.

If you are really struggling, like I was, perhaps one of your support crew will read you excerpts, or a friend might share a snippet they heard.

Many days you may not need this book, but it is here when you are looking for guidance or reassurance.

This is not a story about winning, or the occurrence of a miracle – although I urge you to always think miracles are possible, for the purpose of liberating your aspirations. I aimed as high as I could visualise, and I fell a fraction short. How far short is unclear as I am still chasing those physical improvements, and it is not a journey measured simply in physical outcomes. I have learned much about myself and others over the course of my journey. I am stronger.

Because it is not about the fall – it is about how we choose to get up. It is not about the inertia and the fear – it is how we choose to move, to tackle our fears and embrace uncertainty.

Mine is the journey of an average person, with an above-average support crew, who strived for an exceptional outcome. I know that your support crew will step up too, because those close to you desperately want the best for you. I assure you there will be a breadth of help that you cannot possibly imagine as you read this. It is there, and it is powerful. Together with your own mindset, that support will enable you to become a fraction stronger, every day.

Part I

LANT-ERNS

Light abounds in every heartbeat,
if we are brave enough to see.
Rays of potential in what might come,
the memories of what has been.
Hopes, dreams, summits and falls,
our embers, our hearth, our core.
Our private pilot light – inside, on call,
with kindling to generate more.
This sustaining glow of our embers,
and our freedom to explore what can be,
encourages us onto that enabling path
of embracing uncertainty.

One of my most enduring childhood memories is the day we bought a modestly sized colour TV set on wheels. I recall reception issues and parents who felt that the commercial networks only televised 'trash' that could expose my brother and me to thought pollution. Apart from *The Goodies*, followed by *Doctor Who* and the daily evening news, our TV was seldom on. And it was anchored on channel 2 – the Australian Broadcasting Corporation (ABC).

One show I vividly remember is the mini-series *I Can Jump Puddles*, which brought Australian author Alan Marshall's story to life. Alan contracted polio when the epidemic swept through Victoria in the early 1900s, leaving him crippled from six years of age. Polio invades the nervous system, destroying the nerve cells that control muscles. Its most common impact is leg functionality, but understanding of the disease was limited back then. It was often incorrectly associated with mental as well as physical incapacity.

Alan spent 18 months being treated in hospital, then most of his childhood on crutches with steel callipers attached to his legs. His right leg withered from the disease and was eventually amputated.

As a young boy, like Alan, I loved spending time with horses, admiring their strength and beauty. We had paddocks at the end of our street. I would ride my bike up there most days, with carrots or other treats, spending time patting the horses through the fence and talking to them. I read books like *The Black Stallion* and was over the moon when that story was adapted for the screen. I wanted to be a jockey.

Mum would cart my brother and I off to weekly riding lessons, which worked out badly for everyone. Mum raced around to get us there and spent precious money on expensive lessons for her treasured sons. My older brother, Peter, had little – if any – interest in riding, but was dragged along for efficiency.

I suspect this love of horses is part of why I connected so closely to Alan's story. He was told it was impossible to ride a horse without the use of his legs. But he loved riding, so he taught himself how. He had to refine his sense of balance to counteract his physical deficiencies – the loss of sensory feedback and control from his legs. He broke his challenge into more achievable stages. First just a walk, until he had that mastered. Then a canter, then finally a gallop. It was uplifting to see Alan racing across a paddock on Starlight with a beaming smile of freedom on his face. His goal achieved. One of his passions regained.

Alan's story reminds me that we can always attain moments of joy, embers of normality, even in the toughest of circumstances.

Alan showed remarkable spirit. He consistently achieved milestones considered impossible for someone with almost no leg function. I loved a song from around that time – presumably inspired by the mini-series – which I would sing, especially if I felt lonely or I was facing something difficult. Mum sang it too, encouraging her sons to take on the world:

I can jump puddles, I can jump puddles, I can do anything
I guess if I tried, I could catch a butterfly on the wing.

When I was looking for hope and inspiration in those difficult days in hospital, my memories of Alan Marshall's stories are some I relived. I also thought of my wife's incredible grace and fortitude during her cancer battle, and other friends who had overcome or persevered through life-threatening conditions. I recalled a photograph I had seen of Australian swimming star Karni Liddell – taken when she was a toddler, strapped into some home exercise equipment – and thought about her ability to succeed despite physical challenges. I visualised faceless people in predicaments tougher than I was in, who bravely tackled whatever adversity they faced. People who committed effort to pursue the impossible. People who were undeterred by the uncertainty of their journey.

Those billions of people who are tackling adversity each day visualise – like Alan did – what might be possible. They find the lanterns to guide their mindset. You can visualise exceptional outcomes, too, using lanterns to guide you.

Lanterns light our targets, encouraging us to take those difficult first steps from our current situation. Lanterns are a guidance system, supporting us as we step into uncertainty. Lanterns are inside and all around us, providing light from our memories, our friendships and our purpose. Lanterns connect to our identity and provide the energy and intent to achieve positive change.

Lanterns will help you find and navigate those pathways to your possible.

Chapter 1

Finding your brave face

'Having courage does not mean that we are unafraid.
Having courage and showing courage mean we face our fears.
We are able to say "I have fallen, but I will get up."'

– Maya Angelou

When I was lying in the ditch, gasping for air, I knew it was serious. I could feel that my body was in deep shock, with almost every muscle tense and contracted. I remember commenting, 'Geez it feels bad, boys; I don't think I am flying to Salt Lake City tonight', and hearing from one of the physios with me, 'You never know Berro, it could be just muscular'. All I could think was – you would not say that if you knew what I am experiencing.

My lower back hurt so intensely I cannot recall feeling any other pain. But not for one second did I contemplate that I might have a fractured back or the cleaving consequences of spinal cord damage. Not even when Dave gently took off my shoes and asked, 'Can you wiggle your toes?' Fortunately, I could. But the sensory feedback was vague and distant, which I brushed off as being due to the searing pain I was feeling and the heavy sensation of pins and needles I felt in my legs.

For the most part I was in my own little zone as I lay on my side in that ditch. Overwhelmed, I was just trying to get through each moment; I was in preservation mode, I later realised, even though there was not any risk to my life. Talking was extremely uncomfortable, but I was desperate to escape the gravity of my circumstance, so I attempted occasional moments of humour as we waited the 20 or more minutes for the ambulance to arrive.

I can't recall any thoughts about why the pain was so severe, or that there might be longer-term consequences. I just knew that it felt serious, and I may have some internal injury. I was scared but trying not to show it. I also suppressed the sense of shame I felt that I had crashed; I loved riding and was proud of my skill. I felt confusion as I relived the moments of the crash. What caused the bike to understeer? Why did the front wheel feel so strange through my hands in those moments, as if it were a surfboard caught in a breaking wave and I couldn't pull it free from the surge?

Most of all, I was battling three tiers of guilt:

1. I'd disrupted our ride.
2. I was going to let my colleagues down.
3. I was going to be an inconvenience to my wife that day and perhaps some days beyond.

I instinctively knew I had no chance of being cleared to travel on my flight to LAX at 9.30 that evening, so I was processing my travel alternatives based on what I recalled of the forward flight schedules. I knew there were no Virgin flights on the Monday, but if I could make the Tuesday morning flight then I could arrive in Salt Lake City late Tuesday morning, USA time. I'd only be a few hours late to the workshop. I could still make a meaningful contribution and be there to support the follow-up work. Certainly, I'd be a bit slow and sore, but better to arrive and not completely let the team down. I acknowledge that these thoughts of making an aeroplane flight seem ridiculous in hindsight – but having a problem to focus on certainly helped distract me and get me through the minutes.

What does bravery mean to you?

Do you classify yourself as courageous? I certainly have never thought of myself as brave.

Courage is something we put on a pedestal. The stuff of heroes. Moments of sacrifice or stoic resolve celebrated in timeless movies or songs. I think of Vincent Lingiari, an Australian Indigenous stockman who led a nine-year protest to regain his people's land rights. His brave story is beautifully captured in Kev Carmody and Paul Kelly's song 'From Little Things Big Things Grow'. I think of Peter Weir's film *Gallipoli*. I think of courage in the face of oppression, like in *Cry Freedom*, *The Power of One*, *Mississippi Burning*, *Selma*, *Schindler's List*, *The Zookeeper's Wife* and so many other books and films that have moved me.

For me, bravery is also the type of unyielding resolve shown by Australian Football League (AFL) Hall of Fame player Nigel Lappin, who desperately wanted to play in the Brisbane Lions' 2003 'three-peat' Grand Final, despite fracturing ribs the week before. To be declared fit to play, the day before the game Lappin was put through a fitness test that teammate Jonathan Brown described as 'the most brutal thing I've ever seen'. The coach kicked the ball to Lappin, who was spear tackled by a teammate. This happened repeatedly – perhaps 20 times. Lappin wouldn't give in and was eventually passed fit to play the game. I had flown from Brisbane to Melbourne to watch the game and recall my surprise when I heard he was playing, and then my anxiety as he was 'roughed up' by the opposition in the first minutes of the game. Lappin didn't yield. He was among his team's best players that day, running hard as he always did – perhaps 16 km in the two-hour game – while absorbing intense physical contact. His courage inspired the team to a historic win. After the game Lappin went straight to hospital and spent three days recovering – it was discovered he had played the game with a punctured lung.

These are the type of events I visualise when I think of courage.

I also see bravery in many everyday moments – people asking difficult questions, or holding strong to their values or opinions in the face of prevailing views.

Since my accident, my view has broadened further. Bravery should be whatever you need it to be to help you believe. Whatever gets you through those moments in a ditch and back onto your pins, no matter how long that takes. Or if that extent of recovery proves impossible, to find new meaning – however you manage to define that.

I don't think bravery is something we can plan for; we just need to find our own way to persist in the moment. I doubt Nigel Lappin was trying to be celebrated for being courageous. He was just trying to get through the match – through a series of moments – to achieve his goal. It is only with the benefit of reflection that we can see the magnitude of what has been achieved.

When you allow yourself to reflect, you can find evidence of your own bravery, like I did. In my sporting contests – I always put my body on the line when it counted. At work – pushing through anxiety while preparing for or during a big negotiation, a tense presentation or a conflict I didn't seek but couldn't avoid. I knew I always found ways to confront fear, even if occasionally it took time for me to gather myself for the contest. I was able to persevere through those tough moments. I might have called this grit – a deep determination to fight my way through to the result I desired, because I believe there is courage in being gritty. As leadership writer Margaret M. Perlis says, 'Courage helps fuel grit; the two are symbiotic, feeding into and off of each other'.

I was prepared to lead. Leadership requires, and builds, courage.

In the aftermath of my crash, I wasn't trying to achieve anything apart from just finding a way to get through each moment – consistent with most acts of courage. I distinctly remember the last few minutes before the paramedics arrived particularly testing my resolve to hang on. The pain was truly off the scale, like every nerve was screaming. My body was physically contracted, but my fear was expanding. The wail of the ambulance siren seemed to hang in the air forever. More than two years on, as I type this, I can feel just how much emotion – mostly relief – I associate with Mike's words: 'We can see the ambulance now, Berro.'

Hearing this meant I had made it through the first challenge. Congruent with the words of iconic author J.R.R. Tolkien: 'Courage is found in unlikely places.' Getting through this first challenge gave me strength and belief to face the next.

Manoeuvred from the ditch

When they arrived, the paramedics gave me pain relief, assessed and then stabilised me. Then came the challenge of safely getting me out of that ditch.

I needed to be kept stable to protect my spine. But my position across the contour of the drain meant they could not safely get the stretcher straight underneath me. (Specifically it was a 'CombiCarrier', which consists of two lengthwise pieces, making it easier to insert underneath prone patients.) One of the paramedics problem-solved a solution; I recall her explaining her plan to me and thinking, 'Whatever, just get me out of here'. I felt quite defeated by this point, and impatient to get to hospital so that we could work out what was wrong.

Her plan was achieved with the help of my cycling buddies, saving me from a longer wait for a second ambulance crew. They log rolled me, placing half the stretcher under me. They lifted me a few inches, then delicately changed my angle such that the stretcher could fit lengthways down the middle of the ditch. They placed me back down and log rolled me off to reposition the stretcher, rolled me back on, then combined the two parts of the stretcher with me on it. Once I was secure, the cycling crew carried me about 30 metres downstream, finding a safe place to climb out of the stormwater drain before carting me back to the ambulance.

You can imagine my sense of gratitude for the paramedics' work when I had the story retold to me in those first few fragile days in hospital, and the emotion I felt when I wrote my thanks to them many weeks later. Their care and skill were crucial in me being able to achieve the mobility I have today.

Grasping for meaning through the pain

As we sped towards the hospital, the paramedic travelling with me warned that my wedding ring would be cut off unless I removed it before we reached emergency. I asked if I would cause more damage by dragging it through the deep lacerations he had described on that knuckle. The paramedic said, 'Perhaps, but it looks such a mess I am sure they will need to stitch that finger anyway'. He asked if I wanted his help to sit up a little, to see what I needed to pull the ring through, to which I replied, 'Only if it is going to make the task easier by looking'. It was not, so I just lay back and pulled hard.

My wedding ring was a tight fit and getting it over my knuckle was always a challenge, requiring force and twisting in equal measure. Dragging and twisting it through the torn tissue and skin was awful – it felt like I was tearing myself, taking skin with the ring. I clenched my teeth at the stabbing pain as the ring pressed on exposed nerves as I dragged it off. It was the first of many tests of resolve, but in that moment, I just did not want the wedding ring destroyed on top of my other damage. It was like it was the first battleground of keeping my identity whole, even though I had no idea of how true that thought would prove to be in the coming hours.

Getting through the first few hours following my accident required that same resolve. I needed to just brace and find a way to get through. I utilised that same brave face again many times over the course of my recovery, finding a way to avoid defeat in the hope of better times ahead. Finding courage in the moment and over a sustained – often seemingly infinite – period ahead. Finding the will to persevere.

I found the brave face that allowed me to seek and welcome help. I had to become comfortable with a deeper, more profound, brave face – one that would give me the courage to step into uncertainty, to liberate possibility, to pursue aspirational outcomes and to tackle my fears. It was this infinite brave face that gave me the fortitude to look for the embers of normality that connected me to my identity, that gave me the self-motivation to sustain an effort that had no guarantee of success but was integral to who I wanted to be as a character.

I made the choice on that first day that I could and would improve. And with help from others, I sustained that belief with all my stamina.

I made that choice with inspiration from the bravery I had seen and wanted to see in myself. In people like my wife, and the courage she had continually demonstrated during eight months of sickening chemotherapy. Sustained bravery like that of my dad, John, embodied in his ability to get back up when life had knocked him down.

The battle to keep that brave face

John was the eldest of Bill and Ethel's three children. Bill had an important job as a cage-winder driver in a Kalgoorlie gold mine, until he became deeply affected by a tragic work accident and couldn't continue his role. This stress probably contributed to his early passing – and so it was that at age nine John was called from his North Kalgoorlie classroom by the headmaster and told: 'Your dad is dead. You better go home, son.'

Ethel was always stoic and found a way to make ends meet with very little. She ironed and gained support from Legacy, an Australian non-profit organisation that provides support to veterans' families. The family ran chickens and John would often shoot rabbits and kangaroos with his cherished school mate Ron, providing valuable extra meat for the household.

John took odd jobs, bringing in additional money to support the family and his education. Ethel didn't drive, so John rode his bicycle everywhere. At age 12 John came home holding a handful of his front teeth, having knocked them out when he accidentally rode his bicycle into a pole. 'I was blinded by the sun', he told his mum. Some years after the accident, when the family savings enabled it, it was off to the dentist and the remaining top teeth were pulled out – without anaesthetic – and John's false teeth cast.

John secured a teaching bursary, which assisted him through senior school. He captained the school hockey team and starred as Marco in *The Gondoliers* – a proud part of his regular association with school and local theatre productions. Then it was on to the University of Western Australia, where John made his family so proud by attaining a Bachelor of Science degree, becoming the family's first university graduate. His first teaching post was at Mt Barker Senior High School in 1964, where he was quickly claimed by Beth, who was already teaching at the local primary school.

John and Beth embarked on a 51-year journey yielding two boys, an assortment of pets, boats, canoes and caravans, and a love of entertaining under handmade pergolas and on patios made of second-hand bricks formed into creative arcs that challenged John's capability with a portable grinder.

Along his life journey, John's career progressed quickly. He was seen as a rising star within the WA education system and was promoted to Senior Master of Mathematics. But his gentle, selfless nature saw him taking too much on his own shoulders, and periods of stress curtailed his career. But John found a way to not let these periods of anxiety and depression affect his family achievements – I am sure all parents can appreciate the fortitude it must have taken to tow a caravan around Australia for six months with two bickering boys in the back seat, reversing it into tight caravan bays in fading light at the end of a long day's drive!

John had to deal with a series of major depressive episodes during a period when this condition was suppressed and misunderstood. He often had to put on his brave face to front up to school during or after one of these challenging periods. I can't imagine how tough that must have been at times, the fear it must have invoked – high-school children at state-run schools are notoriously determined not to demonstrate any empathy!

Not only did John consistently find that brave face that gets us through the moment, he often found his way to the infinite brave face that transforms, with sustained periods of success and peace. But such is the fragile nature of mental health, it was an ongoing exercise of employing both. John sustained his internal grit and courage to achieve an amazing, honourable and rewarding life.

My dad's resilience was one of the first things I thought of when I made my choice to pursue my best possible recovery on the day of my accident. I focused on all the things he had achieved despite his challenges. Because to me, he was a champion handyman – welding, cutting and building. He was a successful hockey player, leader and coach. He made fabulous camping and caravanning holidays possible, fishing in a dinghy in so many WA bays, and minding my uncle's farm without major mishap despite the naughty goats giving us plenty of entertaining memories. And he did it all with a warm smile and a twinkle in his eye, telling a joke or amusing both the listener and himself with some witty word play. Donning a brave face, no matter how hard the inner battle.

I didn't want to be defeated by fear or despair. I wanted to tackle any adversity while demonstrating gratitude and decency to others. Just like he did.

I believe we all have a pilot light of courage quietly burning away inside us. It is fuelled by the inspiration that is happening around us all the time – ordinary people doing extraordinary things. This inner flame is stoked by the nurturing of our family, our work and life experiences, including those we identify as heroic from stories or events.

When it counts, you can be braver than you ever imagined.

If you reflect on your life, you can see that your brave face has marched you through many tough moments so far, and has always been there when you needed it. Trust it, release yourself to step into uncertainty, to try and fail, and let your brave face enable you to liberate possibility.

Become a fraction stronger

- Do you think of yourself as courageous?
- Can you recall a tough moment when you had to reach deep inside to find your brave face? Were you surprised by your strength?
- Would you say you are a determined person? What are some examples of when you have shown this?
- How has your sense of bravery changed as you have grown and developed through life?
- Who is the most courageous person you know? What is inspiring about that person?
- What are some small acts of bravery you have witnessed?

Chapter 2
Embracing uncertainty

'The credit belongs to the man who is actually in the arena…
who at the best knows in the end the triumph of high
achievement, and who at the worst, if he fails, at least fails
while daring greatly, so that his place shall never be with those
cold and timid souls who neither know victory nor defeat.'
– Theodore Roosevelt

At around 10 a.m., following at least nine scans and x-rays, the specialists delivered the news. The impact had crushed two of my vertebrae, dislodging a large segment of fractured vertebra into my spinal cord. My spinal cord had suffered 50 per cent compression. There was evidence of nerve-related damage, especially down my left side. I would be operated on later that day – the medical team would pin rods to five of my vertebrae to support my fractured spine and reduce the pressure on my compressed spinal cord. My only prospects of recovery lay on the other side of a successful operation, and the full extent of my spinal cord damage would be unclear for some time.

Does that make much sense to you? It made little to me. I was in shock and struggling to comprehend the damage, never mind the remedy. What would this mean? How would my legs work at only 50 per cent strength, or even less?

I was shaken. I was desperate not to lose my mobility. My mind was racing. Lucy was so shocked she felt she might no longer be able to hold herself up, so she slid along the wall until she reached the nearest chair.

In that moment, everything was uncertain. Change had been a regular feature of my life – we moved regularly growing up, and I had lived in four cities across three countries as an adult – but nothing compared to this. I found myself confronted by the uncertainty of a fractured body and identity.

Shortly after hearing the devastating prognosis, Lucy left the hospital, facing the difficult task of sharing the news with our kids, the cycling crew, my workmates and other family members including my mum, who was still dealing with the loss of my dad less than two years before.

I found myself alone in hospital. I felt so removed from the hectic activity all around me. I was isolated in my world of uncertainty, reflecting on how – in just a split second – the pathway of my life had become vastly different. Those first few hours alone were the first of many reflective periods for me; I had to find my brave face. I was filled with dread about what lay ahead. Could I recover? If so, to what extent? Did I have the mental strength and depth of character to respond to the challenge? What example would I set for my children and others around me?

Learning to tolerate ambiguity

The accident was not the first opportunity I'd had to cope with change. Like most corporate employees, I've lived through my share of organisational restructures. I was largely comfortable with workplace change. We received corporate training in how to cope with complexity and disruption, how to avoid making false promises to ourselves about future comfort or stability. As a leader, I sought opportunities to constructively challenge existing mindsets and perceived barriers, to liberate improvement opportunities – whether that be financial value or team outcomes – because I enjoyed testing constraints and enhancing outcomes.

The Theodore Roosevelt quote that opens this chapter is powerful, forgiving that it is dated in its gender references. One of my leaders had the quote on their office wall – an office where we had many discussions planning customer proposals and gaining approval for negotiating mandates. When you are dealing with complex sales (those that include multiple stakeholders) and high-value negotiations – as I did for much of my career – you are working with significant ambiguity. I always associate Roosevelt's quote with the willingness to step into uncertainty, to try with intent and purpose. To sometimes fail, but to do so with grace knowing that you have committed to the challenge.

This familiarity with change and ambiguity helped me deal with the extent of the disruption caused by my spinal cord injury. I was desperate to avoid languishing in a pit of despair, so I reframed the uncertainty of my diagnosis and prognosis into thoughts that I could use to give myself hope and focus.

I quickly realised I had to minimise the energy spent seeking to understand what had happened. I did not pursue a perfect understanding of my situation, but rather built a 'good enough' acceptance as quickly as I could. Then I focused on whatever first small steps would move me forward most effectively from that situation.

I felt no urgency to see the x-rays showing the metalwork in my back. The first time I saw the picture of those rods and screws was ten days after my operation, on the day I first tried to walk within the safety of parallel bars. This is when it made sense for the physio to show me – to explain some of my challenges.

It took over a month before I looked at the CT scan of the damage that my accident had done to my vertebrae. I finally realised the crushing damage to my vertebrae and nerves stemmed from my helmet striking the ground. Until that point, I had assumed it was the second thumping impact as I came to rest on my side, because that was the instant the avalanche of pain arrived.

The scans provided a valuable aid for my physios to sharpen my focus on the actions that would help me improve. Understanding the linkage between my injuries and current deficiencies helped me reimagine my recovery at a time when my optimism was waning.

I only ever sought the level of awareness I required at each point of the journey to generate, enhance or replenish my vision of my exceptional outcome. This ensured I focused my effort firmly on moving forward.

The stress of uncertainty

It's normal for us to resist uncertainty. A 2016 study found that it's more stressful for us to know that there is a small chance of getting an electric shock than the certainty of knowing that we will definitely be shocked. Experiments dating back to the 1960s consistently show that people have less of a reaction to experiencing an electric shock when they know it's coming than if it comes as a surprise. We would rather experience an electric shock than deal with the discomfort of knowing a shock may or may not come our way. That's because uncertainty makes it difficult to prepare for events or to control them.

If that's the case, how do we deal with the stress of uncertainty? Organisational psychology researchers Richard Plenty and Terri Morrissey say that taking personal responsibility and focusing on what *can* be done makes a big difference. Harvard Medical School psychologist Ryan Jane Jacoby tells us that dwelling on the past or worrying about the future can be exhausting. If we use deliberate strategies like worry postponement (to a set date) or redirecting our attention by staying active in the moment, then we can reduce the impact of rumination and its negative implications, such as anxiety and depression.

On the day of my crash, I knew I was in a bad way. As I lay waiting for the results of my scans, I can't recall contemplating the words 'spinal cord injury', and I do feel both those initial hours and the journey ahead may have been more difficult had I speculated on or dreaded the extent of my bad news. I believe that the transition from uncertainty (but open to optimism) to shock to hope is a more fluent transition than dread to confirmation to hope.

In outlining my predicament, the specialists provided a clear pathway. Their process was in control, and it was my responsibility to do likewise: to control what I could control by getting my attitude right. To get through that first day in the best shape for the challenges ahead, I had to generate resolve and remain positive, and most of all, trust the medical experts.

The more challenging times were the next few days, when I was lying alone on my hospital bed becoming more aware of the magnitude of uncertainty ahead. The shocks of uncertainty kept coming at me, and I was not enjoying receiving them. First of all, it was the complexity of any movement at all in bed. I was so sore and sorry for myself. I had my left arm in a sling to protect my shoulder, and the whole forearm and hand were bound up in a temporary cast. My right arm had three sets of IV tubes inhibiting its movement. It was nice to receive text messages of support, but I could barely lift my phone to focus on it, so replying was almost impossible and the messages mostly made me feel helpless and scared of what lay ahead.

Most of all, it was the realisation I could barely move my feet and toes. And while I was demonstrating strength in my legs when the specialists were testing my ability to move them – by pulling and pushing on them – I knew my legs were totally ineffective to help me move when I needed to just shuffle myself a couple of centimetres back up the bed.

On that first Monday – the day after the accident – I was sent for follow-up scans to check on the success of my operation. I became exhausted and emotionally deflated by the complexity of being transferred from my hospital bed to the mobile trolley bed using slide sheets and slide boards. They needed two nurses and a 'wardie' to roll and slide me. Despite straining to do so, I was helpless to contribute in any meaningful way.

On the next day, my physiotherapist declared that they were going to stand me up. I was petrified. It was about 32 hours post-operation and I was deeply sore. But my fear wasn't about pain. I had no faith that my legs would be able to take my weight, given how limited in use they were just lying down, and they jerked wildly when I strained to move them. Just the tiniest movement in bed took enormous energy, and I was having dizzy spells every time I substantially changed my position.

I did stand, with the help of two physiotherapists. While this gave me a milestone to celebrate, the muddled sensations on how to move my legs just illuminated the extent of the nerve damage I was so desperately hoping – and trying to convince myself – might be less than the medical team anticipated. It exacerbated that sense of uncertainty.

I realised quickly that focusing on things I couldn't control would only make my recovery more difficult.

Concentrating on what I could control was essential to manage my limited energy and achieve the critical steps of progress identified by the physiotherapists. I needed to apply effort to my crucial actions but keep my awareness of the possibility beyond that. I used my peripheral vision to keep that awareness by remaining curious and optimistic about how, in time, I might grow my control and my sphere of influence. To compare that to my hockey career, I focused on the opponent in front of me but sustained an awareness of the game around me. The opportunity was in the latter, but that was irrelevant if I lost focus on the former.

I elected to embrace the uncertainty rather than let it constrain me. I tried to accept that making long-term goals might be difficult today, but if I could get through today, this week and next month, my world would shift. What I'd felt I needed to know yesterday might have no relevance in my future, so worrying about it was a pointless waste of my precious energy.

The same can be said for any type of uncertainty you may be facing. We have experienced tremendous global disruption during 2020 and 2021 due to the COVID-19 pandemic. But most acutely, disruption and uncertainty is personal – navigating the passing of a loved one, the fear of losing your job, the devastation of a fractured relationship or the impacts of a global disruption on your life routines and plans. Strengthening your ability to tolerate that uncertainty is integral to your resilience, and success. It is too easy to overlook all the cherished things that uncertainty has brought us and focus on our concerns. Yoshida Kenkō captures this beautifully in the quote, 'The most precious thing in life is its uncertainty'.

A new perspective

Embracing uncertainty allows you to liberate possibility. It broadens the range of possible outcomes that you can visualise and target. It changes your perspective: suddenly you are looking outwards at the world. You see the potential to improve and feel positive about pursuing that improvement. You have released yourself to try. You have uncovered a broader horizon of possibilities.

Embracing uncertainty is powerful in two ways. Firstly, it allows you to find acceptance. You're probably familiar with the five stages of grief, as proposed by Elisabeth Kübler-Ross in the 1960s. In her model, acceptance is the point of resolution that allows people to move forward and find meaning in their circumstances. If we can live with a 'good enough' level of acceptance – by tolerating uncertainty – we reach acceptance quicker, enabling us to move forward.

Secondly, tolerating uncertainty broadens the horizon of possibility. Think about it in reverse: if we avoid uncertainty, we constrain the infinite nature of possibility.

By tolerating uncertainty, you give yourself permission to try, to fail. To commit. To act and benefit from the consequences of that action. Lean in to the unknown; it is often more valuable to act now than to wait for perfect information or acceptance to arrive.

The power of not knowing

A week after my accident, my mate Steely visited me in hospital. He shared the story of his niece, Ellen – a woman who overcame a similar injury and operation to my own in the face of immense uncertainty. This story helped me believe in my ability to step up to the challenge. It provides a great example of focusing on what you can control. I want to share Ellen's story with you in the hope that you'll feel the same sense of inspiration that I did from her ability to navigate uncertainty.

Ellen was halfway through a dream holiday in Egypt. She spent her first week seeing the pyramids, Aswan and the Valley of the Kings. Ancient history had always fascinated her, so she loved seeing all these ruins. Her overnight Nile River sailing experience on a felucca boat was another highlight. For her second week, Ellen was headed to Dahab to enjoy its golden sands and world-class scuba diving, and to hike rugged Mt Sinai.

About 5 a.m. on Sunday morning, on the outskirts of Cairo, Ellen's tour bus inadvertently hit a speedbump – hard. People and items were propelled from their resting places. Ellen was asleep. The position of her legs under the seat in front may have contributed to the way the impact jarred her spine as the bus slammed down. That instant of intense pain drew a sharp scream in the same blinking of an eye that she was jolted awake. And then she was gasping for breath, her lung function shallowed by shock and pain. She did not know what had happened, just that it hurt so deeply. She felt searing shockwaves of pain.

A fellow tourist, a nurse, leapt to Ellen's aid. She calmed Ellen and carefully moved her into the recovery position on her seat. They all waited to see if the pain settled and her breath recovered. It did not.

There was a hospital just five minutes away, so they decided to take Ellen there to be checked over.

Lost in translation

Lying on a bed in the emergency department, having been scanned and x-rayed, Ellen started to feel a bit brighter. Her natural colouring started to reclaim her face from that washed-out whiteness of pain and shock. She was starting to believe her holiday could be back on track soon.

Then the doctor told Ellen, the message translated into English by one of the tour guides, that she had a vertebra fracture. She was asked not to move. While the seriousness of her situation was perhaps lost in translation, it was clear to Ellen that her holiday was not going to be back on track soon. She calmly started to telephone for help: her travel insurance, her mum. She took photos of the x-rays and sent them to her mum, who started seeking guidance from the family's network in Brisbane. A friend knew an orthopaedic surgeon, who looked at the scans. Advice was swiftly relayed back to Ellen, via her family, that her situation was perilous. She was at risk of spinal cord damage. She was going to require surgery before coming home.

Ellen had never broken a bone before. Extraction of her wisdom teeth was the extent of her prior patient experience. The idea of back surgery triggered fear, but her mum's calming voice helped her through that moment.

Seeking help via the Australian embassy in Cairo and her travel insurance company, Ellen received support and safe transfer to a private hospital while arrangements were made for where her spinal surgery would be performed.

She learned her surgery would take place in Hamburg, Germany, and she would be transferred via air ambulance the following day (Monday). Her dad would fly to Hamburg from Australia to be with her.

Just get through

Monday arrived – and so did a sandstorm. It wasn't safe for the air ambulance to fly.

Then Hamburg caught a flu epidemic, so there was no longer a bed for Ellen there. Instead, there was a possibility she might be transferred to a Canadian military hospital in Dubai, or to Vienna.

Through all this uncertainty, Ellen's mum, her family and the communication from her insurance provider combined to keep Ellen calm.

'I knew my family were doing everything they could, and that my dad was on the way. I just had to do my part: to get through it, to get to the next step.'

By Wednesday she learned that a bed had been secured in Vienna. Her dad was still on his way to Hamburg.

One of the tour leaders stayed with her 9 a.m. to 5 p.m. for her days in hospital, providing translation support. On the Wednesday Ellen was told that the hospital in Vienna requested she have an MRI performed in Cairo, so it could be uploaded to them in preparation for Ellen's operation. She waited for the MRI all day, but it didn't eventuate.

That night she was woken in the middle of the night – perhaps around 2 a.m. No-one spoke English so there was no explanation as to why she had been woken or why she was being prepared to be moved somewhere. Ellen was loaded into an ambulance and taken to a separate building for her MRI to be performed.

It was bizarre, but Ellen just trusted the process. She tolerated the uncertainty.

> 'When I look back, I think I should have been much more terrified about these things – but the not knowing was almost helpful. Maybe the language barrier actually helped too.'

Meanwhile, Ellen's dad arrived in Hamburg and learned he would need to travel to Vienna the next day.

En route to Vienna

On the Thursday morning Ellen was taken to the airport by ambulance and put on an air ambulance. She arrived in Vienna early afternoon and was transferred to the trauma hospital where her operation was scheduled to be performed.

On arrival she was put through a full bio-check because she had been travelling in Africa. Until that was cleared, she was treated by doctors and nurses in full personal protective equipment.

> 'I just tried to stay focused. It was hard enough for mum, that this was happening to her daughter overseas. I just had to keep going and not make it worse for her.'

The first doctor that came to brief Ellen explained the x-rays to her. He conveyed how serious the damage was and how close she had come to spinal cord damage. He assured her that they had it under control. Perhaps it was the proximity of the hospital to ski fields, but Ellen sensed that the hospital had a lot of experience in handling this type of injury. Hearing explanations directly from a doctor in English certainly helped provide reassurance, too!

Once she had reached her hospital room, she was told she could move around so long as she was careful. Ellen will never forget the pleasure of that first shower or the joy of being reunited with her dad. 'We were both pretty emotional. I don't see Dad emotional very often. So that was really nice.'

Ellen learned surgery had been scheduled for Wednesday. They would put a fixation in her spine to stabilise it, protect the fractured vertebra from weight bearing and eliminate the risk of the fractured piece impacting her spinal cord.

The big day

As Ellen was wheeled out for the operation, she had her second hit of fear. It was stronger than the fear caused by that painful jolt ten days before – she was suddenly terrified.

But the operation was a success, all over in 90 minutes, and Ellen was transferred to recovery. Unfortunately, no-one told Ellen's dad. He waited for six or seven hours in Ellen's room before finding out the operation had been a success when his daughter was rolled into the room!

The next morning, her nurses told Ellen she would have to start moving.

'I will never forget how painful that was. They rotated me onto my side, and then I had to lift my body up with their help to sit on the side of the bed. I had this awful pulling pain on my back muscles – it was excruciating.'

Ellen was tested by the neurologist for sensory or physical losses and given the wonderful news that all was normal. Her ability to hang in there, to face uncertainty and trust the process, had paid off.

An exceptional recovery

Ellen and her dad flew home to Brisbane. It was exhausting, especially transiting between flights, but she was home and on the road to recovery. Her spinal fixation was removed 18 months later. She has had no long-term impacts – an exceptional outcome made possible by the care of that nurse on the bus, support from many people, love from Ellen's family and, crucially, Ellen's ability just to focus on that next step. She was never distracted by the amplitude of the uncertainty she was navigating.

Ellen's resolve enabled her to do her part – to get through the tough moments, to get to the next step.

The window Steely provided me into Ellen's story helped me do it, too. So can you.

Embracing uncertainty is a lantern to live your life by. Understand that disruption is common, and moments of uncertainty – big and small – affect all of us. Some of this is seen, but most is unseen.

In my recovery I was forced to accept the uncertainty of my situation and the inherent risks. Despite change having been a regular feature of my life before the accident, my fractured body and identity brought uncertainty to a whole new level. In just a fraction of a second, the pathway ahead of me had become littered with fear and uncertainty.

Navigating that ambiguity reinforced the adage that a problem shared is a problem halved. But sharing problems alone does not move you forward – you must decide and act. Loosen that need for control and you will liberate your capacity to accept and dream.

Embrace the fear of stepping into the unknown. Because once you do, you will pave the way to new possibilities.

Become a fraction stronger

- Have you experienced a disruptive event or period of time that plunged you into uncertainty? How did that make you feel?
- What action did you take in response to that disruption?
- How did that decision to take action affect how you felt about the situation? Did you feel more anxious and uncertain, or less?
- What opportunities did you gain from living through the uncertain situation?

Chapter 3
Liberating possibility

'The future is completely open and we are writing it
moment to moment.'
– Pema Chödrön

On that first morning, in the moments when I was processing the doctors' words, it was difficult to visualise best possible outcomes. My most vivid memory is of hearing the words '50 per cent compression' of my spinal cord. This cut deep into my identity. *What will life be like? Will I be independent? Will it impact my ability to participate in my children's lives in the way I love doing now? In the way I hoped to do in the future?*

I was shocked and devastated.

Suddenly it felt like all the things that I treasured about my life had just been snatched away. I lived an active life. I loved participating in sport and immersing myself in the beauty of nature. The travel plans I had for my future might just be too difficult. I felt incredible sorrow and guilt – that for my remaining years, I might be a burden to my beautiful family.

My specialists did not provide any hope for a full recovery when they explained the urgent operation planned for later that day. They would insert two 230 mm rods and fix them to five of my vertebrae using ten 5.5 mm–diameter screws. To visualise this, think about two solid metal straws spread a few centimetres apart, aligned vertically down the middle of your back. Clamps allow these metal straws to be fixed to your spine using screws 40 to 45 mm long. Think about a standard pencil. Snap it into four equal pieces. These are about the dimensions of the screws that were driven deep into my vertebrae to fix the rods in place.

Urgently stabilising my spine was my only viable recovery pathway. If operating was successful, as they expected, I would avoid further damage and functional loss. But the damage that had already occurred would not be alleviated. The specialists prepared me for a long and difficult challenge to walk again, and said that would likely include compromised mobility – perhaps even walking aids.

My mind was racing: *how can I overcome this?*

Visualising the possible

As I processed the doctors' words, I knew I had to find a way to regain hope. I had to seek out the areas of ambiguity in what I had heard and try to find pathways to the positives – to create a thought process that enabled me to reframe the uncertainty into my best possible outcomes. I developed and latched onto the thought that if every spinal cord injury is unique, so every recovery can be unique.

I drew my own probability curve between the prognosis and the absolute best possible outcome I could imagine.

I started by visualising myself retaining independence by getting around, even if my mobility was heavily compromised as I had just heard it likely would be. *It will be inconvenient, but I will find a way to get around.*

Then I told myself that the doctors only have a perception of what the range of outcomes could be, based on their experience and what they have read. Sure, it is a sensible, informed view, but that is not the whole sample of outcomes. And they need to be a little conservative to manage expectations. So, I visualised a world where I made a full recovery, even though this was well beyond the prognosis.

To achieve exceptional results, we must be able to picture them.

I resolved that my every action must be aimed at making sure I at least fell between those two points: the confronting prognosis and my imagined recovery. This gave me a sliver of hope. I reasoned that, with focus and perseverance, I might hit that best edge.

With time and effort, I strengthened my vision of making that full recovery. But I also regularly counselled myself not to make false promises about the likelihood of that upside. I acknowledged that I would probably fall short – but there would always be some possibility. And I targeted that possibility, no matter how slim, because I needed that upside to focus my determination, to support the attitude that I wanted to generate and sustain as part of demonstrating my character.

I told myself that I had two targets: the outcomes that I wanted, and the attitude that I wanted. Even if I fell short of the outcomes – which were not in my control – I could still achieve and be proud of my attitude, which was in my control.

The power of possibility

If you have not heard of him already, let me introduce you to Indigenous Australian musician Dr G. Yunupingu (known in life as Gurrumul). He was born in Galiwin'ku (Elcho Island), about 580 kilometres east of Darwin, off the coast of Arnhem Land. Even by Australian standards, this community is extremely remote.

Yunupingu taught himself how to play an accordion at four years old and the guitar at five. He was left-handed but only had access to a right-handed guitar, so he learned to play holding the guitar upside down. He left school at 12 years of age.

Yunupingu was born blind. He didn't much like braille. But he pursued his musical passion: leaving his remote home, becoming part of the Australian band Yothu Yindi and co-writing their timeless anthem 'Treaty'. He co-founded Saltwater Band. He released 4 solo albums. He won 6 Australian Independent Record (AIR) Awards, 2 Australasian Performing Right Association (APRA) Music Awards, 9 Australian Recording Industry Association (ARIA) Awards and 22 National Indigenous Music Awards.

Against all odds, Yunupingu unfolded an amazing myth that will live on though his music. The Pema Chödrön quote that opens this chapter should arouse our inner Yunupingu – to encourage us that almost anything is possible. It stirs us to embrace uncertainty by not being satisfied with the constraints of the known. To stretch for our dreams no matter how difficult or distant they seem. To identify and strive for that broad horizon of possibility.

Many things prove to be possible that we initially dismiss or cannot foresee. Just picture for a moment some of the technology shifts of the last 150 years – the internet, cars, planes, putting a man on the moon and a drone on Mars, just to name a few. All these developments illustrate that incredible things can happen if we exercise our mental agility. Former South African President Nelson Mandela, one of the world's most revered leaders, sums it up perfectly: 'It always seems impossible until it's done.'

The Australian television series *Redesign My Brain*, starring television presenter Todd Sampson, follows Todd in his quest to expand the boundaries of his brain with the assistance of experts and specific exercises. The first season honed Todd's mental capabilities towards a final challenge in which he had to escape from being chained, handcuffed and blindfolded underwater. Quite a traumatic test for someone who can't swim! The second season prepared Todd for a daunting high-wire walk between two buildings – 21 floors above the ground.

The premise behind the series is that mental training – via specific actions and visualisation – has the power to change the physical structure and performance of our brain. Research supporting this premise includes a 2003 Harvard study in which two groups of people were asked to practise a five-finger piano exercise. One group physically practised, while the other was asked to just visualise themselves playing instead of physically playing. The experiment demonstrated that the brain was stimulated in the same way for both groups.

In 2010, the BBC created a mini-series based on the Harvard 'counter-clockwise' research of Professor Ellen Langer – an experiment that tested whether reliving your youth could make you young again.

In Professor Ellen's landmark 1981 study, a group of elderly men were immersed in a retreat created to reflect daily life in the 1950s for one week. Men in a 'control' group were told to stay in the present and simply reminisce about that era. The 'experimental' group were asked to pretend they were young men, once again living in the 1950s. The experimental group showed greater improvement in vision, strength, joint flexibility, finger length (their arthritis diminished and they could straighten their fingers more) and manual dexterity. On intelligence tests, 63 per cent of the experimental group improved their scores, compared to 44 per cent of the control group.

In the BBC series, six British celebrities were sent back to 1975 by recreating the world they had left behind 35 years ago. The participants agreed to live in '1975' for one week. They dressed in 1970s clothes, slept in replicas of their very own 1970s bedrooms, watched television from that era and talked about 1975 in the present tense.

Just as Professor Ellen had discovered all those years before, the BBC saw great changes. Halfway through the week's test, one participant – who always walked with two walking sticks and often relied on a wheelchair – took 148 steps with the aid of just one walking stick. By the end of the week, memory, mood, flexibility, stamina and even eyesight had improved in almost all participants – in some cases they shed up to 20 years of their apparent biological age.

Allow yourself to wonder

This research encourages us to never underestimate the powerful beacon of possibility, a concept that is beautifully described in Amanda Gorman's US presidential inauguration poem 'The Hill We Climb', encouraging us that:

> *The new dawn blooms as we free it*
> *for there is always light*
> *if only we're brave enough to see it.*

Every moment has the potential to change your life. Will an external trigger be your catalyst? Will a thought inside you ignite your motivation? In either respect, I urge you to believe in the possible and act to pursue it.

Amanda's verse tells us there is always light. She encourages us to step into uncertainty, to be brave. Empower yourself to try. Visualise your possibilities.

Amanda inspires me to wonder. Wondering helps me to explore, and to inquire, to project an image of what I want to achieve. I wasn't thinking of research as I lay in hospital. I was tapping into my sense of wonder, to find any positive way out of my predicament. I was using the experiences I had gained in life and work to visualise and target my most exceptional outcomes to give myself the best possible chance of a meaningful recovery. And at that point – rightly or wrongly – picturing a meaningful recovery was central to my sense of worth.

Protecting your vision of the possible

My wife was influential in protecting my vision of the best possible outcomes, with one simple condition as she handed me my phone on that first morning: 'Do not google your injuries.' I promise you, on that first morning I had absolutely no desire to google anything, but perhaps in the hours or days that followed I could have. Lucy's wisdom stopped me scrolling for greater certainty that could have been wrong and almost certainly would have constrained my vision of the possible. She helped me focus my precious energy on the unconstrained potential of 'my journey, my outcomes'.

Subsequently, friends who had also been through traumatic events conveyed the same message – googling was unhelpful at best, often just heightened fear, and increased their exposure to 'victim mentality'.

I am grateful that Lucy provided her guidance. It protected my possible.

Possibility should be infinite. Allow that full range of possibilities – don't constrain it. What might seem impossible today may change with time, with some effort, some progress, even with a setback! Our perspectives and knowledge change as we try, as we progress, as we fail, altering what seems possible.

The more you broaden the range of what is possible, the stronger your sense of hope becomes. Accept that what you are striving for may never be achievable because it is at the edge of possible, but remember that, as you progress, you are constantly refining what is possible. It is a vision, not a goal.

My journey reminds us that no matter how bleak things feel in any given moment, there is always a range of possible outcomes. As soon as you can, visualise yourself at the best edge of that range, and hold onto that hope for as long as it lasts. Listen carefully to the experts and visualise what else might be possible. Listen to your body, to your loved ones, and to the specialists.

Willing to try

About ten years before my crash, I had the opportunity to hear Karni Liddell speak. Karni was born with a rare neuromuscular wasting disease and was not expected to live past her teenage years. Instead, she set a world record at 14 years of age and became one of Australia's most successful Paralympic swimmers. I am grateful that elements of her story are embedded into my memory and came flashing back in those first hours when I was desperately hunting belief.

When Karni was 12 months old, her parents were told she had been born with spinal muscular atrophy. Their precious first child would never crawl or walk. They were encouraged to let her do as little activity as possible to protect her muscles from deterioration.

Her doting parents had other ideas. They started what Karni describes as her 'crazy rehab program'. It began with a home-made standing frame, which she was strapped into. This was soon mounted onto wheels, and her mother would walk her around for hours in that contraption.

Then Karni's dad built a harness system that allowed her to walk by herself. She underwent physio and massage, cycling, swimming and trampolining exercises, which all had a positive impact. With her parents' unwavering encouragement and support, Karni walked at the age of three and a half.

Against all odds, Karni attended an able-bodied school and did her best to participate in normal life. She embraced the challenge as almost every child does – without reservations – especially with respect to sporting events.

When Karni was eight, her mum entered her in a 25-metre freestyle swimming race as part of an event for disabled children. Karni had never swum 25 metres, and she could not lift her arms above her head because of her muscular disease. She battled to make the distance – it took nearly five minutes – but she got a blue ribbon. First!

Karni felt good. She had excelled at something, when most of her life so far had felt like a struggle to keep up. She chose to be a swimmer. Her parents celebrated with her and encouraged her. They built on that positive feeling.

Karni represented Australia at two Paralympic Games, winning two freestyle bronze medals. She was team captain at the 2000 Summer Paralympics in Sydney. She became an ambassador for people with disability, and was awarded a Pride of Australia Medal. She became an internationally acclaimed keynote speaker.

She has inspired millions of people through her actions and her words. One of her statements I connect deeply with is this: 'Hope is the most powerful gift, the most powerful ingredient you can ever add to a person's life... you can never underestimate the difference one person can make to another person's life.'

Karni's parents liberated possibilities with their hope, with their willingness to lean into the unknown – possibilities that Karni pursued with all her willpower, achieving exceptional outcomes. You made a difference to my life, Karni Liddell.

Possibility and uncertainty are intertwined. By embracing uncertainty, you let possibility be infinite. By keeping an open mind, and pushing yourself outside your comfort zone by being willing to try and fail, you create possibilities that are unforeseen.

I realised that to preserve my energy, I needed to focus my efforts. I had to open the door to possibility by wondering, 'What might I be able to achieve?' I formed a vision of my ideal outcomes, then updated and strengthened that vision as I received new information. By opening my mind to inquiry, I could expand my horizon of possibilities and then refine my vision about what success could look like.

I am convinced that no matter how bleak it feels, there is always a range of possible outcomes. Make a mantra of Sonny Kapoor's famous line from Deborah Moggach's novel *The Best Exotic Marigold Hotel*: 'Everything will be alright in the end, and if it is not alright, it is not the end.' Let it remind you that there is always hope. And applying effort to liberate and pursue that hope – that full horizon of possibilities – is completely in your control.

Become a fraction stronger

- What is the best possible outcome you could hope to achieve despite your current challenge or uncertainty?
- How do you imagine life will be if you're able to achieve that outcome? Can you picture it?
- Can you identify the steps that might lead from your current situation to your ideal outcome? What are they?
- How might you protect your vision of the possible and ensure your sense of hope is maintained?

Chapter 4
Raking your embers

'What if we could call off the search for "the new normal"?
...and learn how to draw on our essence and connectedness
in ways we have never done before?'
– Cassandra Goodman

The day of my accident began a period of transition and self-discovery. Perhaps you can recall similar days of your own. The intensity of a major disruption or loss; the range of emotions you digest your way through; the energy that consumes. Like most transitions, it was not a smooth or direct path. I had periods when certain thoughts and emotions were more dominant: just donning a brave face to start, then being floored by devastating uncertainty, before driving myself to find possibility with all earnest – to stand back up, figuratively speaking, as well as physically. Elements of each of those attitudes were required all the way through those first hours and beyond.

The period of solitude, once Lucy left to tend to our kids, was defining. I felt deflated, confused. Helplessness and loneliness descended on me. I waited for news of my surgery drifting in and out of light sleep, exhausted by the day's events.

I suffered the perturbation of a conscious catheter insertion. I was physically and emotionally wounded. My mind was awash with tears, which seeped out occasionally. I looked at pictures on my phone in our cycling chat group, posted by my crew with no idea of the seriousness of my predicament. I couldn't bear to see the series of photographs of me lying forlorn in the ditch, then being loaded into the ambulance. I looked away as soon as I saw the first one downloading. The photos reinforced my sense of feeling broken.

That solitude dragged me to the depths of despair. It forged steel into my resolve. It generated the willpower I needed to throw everything at my recovery. To prove what I was made of. And the first thing I focused on was connecting to the things that really mattered to me. If all else went to pot, what might make life bearable? I earmarked the core values that I could sustain, such as effort and tenacity. The willingness to face adversity with a smile, even if it was sometimes a fleeting one. I coaxed myself to saddle up for the battle the way that always worked best for me – with conviction, hope and humour.

My first interaction with the world outside of my bubble of pain and uncertainty was at about lunchtime via our cycling chat group, as the crew started responding to a shared update that Lucy had phoned in to Steve. Their messages of support overwhelmed me, and I shed tears of gratitude and self-pity. An hour or two later, once I had found the emotional strength, I responded to the chat.

'Hey boys. Thanks for all the support and care post my entertainment. Really appreciate it. Fractured left wrist, three ribs and two vertebrae seems to be the score so far. Some spinal cord damage, so getting operated on later today once Lucy gets the pins and rods from Bunnings. Mainly left side movement loss issues but of an extent I am hopeful full recovery is possible. Probably not skiing Salt Lake City next weekend though... Berro'

I had tears as I typed this, triggered by the line about appreciation for their support. The moment made me feel gratitude not just for their kind words, but for all the avenues of kindness that had shepherded me to this point of my life and for how fortunate I was to have this common goodness around me, especially when I really needed it.

I struggled to describe the accident – I didn't want to even use that word. I wanted to use 'inconvenience' because of the guilt I felt for holding them up, but I didn't like how that placed more focus on my woes, so I settled on 'entertainment' to lighten it. But I felt a pang of hollow dread as I thumbed out the letters in a one-handed battle with the phone, because I knew the line about 'hopeful full recovery is possible' was completely unrealistic based on what I had heard not long before. I needed to make it feel like it could potentially be OK – it was essential for me to retain and demonstrate hope.

I sent similar messages of optimism to my Rio Tinto colleagues, including my PACE consulting team, who I had been working with for the last 18 months. These messages were about more than just garnering belief: they were supercharged by regret and had extra words to that effect. From the inconvenience of my last-minute-cancelled Salt Lake City flights to the guilt that I would not contribute to the completion of our project and someone would need to carry my load, I felt that I had let them down. I expressed hope I might return part-time to support them in a month or two if the work progressed into its next phases. I cloaked myself in this 'superhuman recovery' façade as I sought to soften that sense of inadvertent abandonment of my duties.

With hindsight, I can see that my ability to convey optimism was aided by an insufficient appreciation of the extent of my injury, as in Ellen's story from chapter 2, where the power of not knowing widened her window of hope. I used humour as a window to my hope and as the drapes for my fragilities.

Find and rake your embers

Finding the funny side may not be your thing. You may not have the same inclination for positivity that I do. Your situation may be more bleak, more complex. Finding the willpower for your journey – be that recovery, reform or growth – may be even tougher or take greater fortitude to initiate. Change was forced upon me – you don't have much choice when parts of your body are mashed up in an instant. It can be harder to instigate and sustain reform without that external trigger. But it can be done; people are doing it around you every minute. I fought to regain momentum many times during my journey, when despair gnawed or belief faded. You can do it too. I am encouraging you to find your own way, your own drivers, in your own time. Draw on your own attributes and uniqueness – your strengths.

When you are faced with a challenge, rekindle your embers of normality through memory and events. Feel their warmth; let them guide you to your possible. Enjoy the visits from family, friends and strangers that take your mind away from hardship for a moment. Give your embers the stoking they need to work their magic on your mindset. Those embers may sometimes be faint, but they are countless in number, and there is such powerful light when embers gather. Their glow will make you stronger, will help you to believe and persevere. Visualise yourself raking all those embers together, combining their glow and heat like the coals in a fire. Relive the magic of how that fire flickers – or even roars – back to life when you give it focus and time.

Find and nurture those embers of normality. Your inner fire. Reminisce. Smile. Try to find the lighter side of moments if that is your thing. But most of all, be you. Think about what is important to you, what stimulates you, and make sure you target thoughts and actions that connect yourself to that sense of identity.

Australian author Janine Shepherd sums this up perfectly: 'A broken body isn't a broken person.' Find the parts of you that are not broken, like your spirit, your intent. This will give you strength in the present as well as providing an important platform for redeveloping your full sense of meaning.

Our embers represent our deep identity, the things that matter most to us and give us stability and purpose. The stuff we can rely on and go to when life gets hard.

And on 10 March 2019, life was hard.

I needed to rake up my embers – all the positive thoughts I could muster about who I was and what I valued. My worth centred on making a positive contribution to family and to my teams – friends, work, community. I thought of all the joy our family created for me and how desperately I wanted to stay connected to their futures. I reflected on the way I had battled through my toughest work periods and the fulfilment that delivered. I recalled how deeply touched I had been when my former boss, Alan, wrote about the high-value outcomes I'd achieved during periods of intense pressure and industry upheaval.

Alan described an enduring contribution delivered by leading with composure, good humour and humility. Recognising the worthiness inherent in 'how we front up' – as a key part of our overall achievements – provides foundations for our sense of being. Alan's words captured many of my most important embers. They reminded me how deeply I valued my positive attitude, including using a sense of fun to diffuse pressure, to fuel my determination to endure and succeed. I knew I could do it again.

Stoke your embers

There is recurring emotional fragility involved in navigating disruption and loss – at least there is for me. I had to keep finding ways to release those anxieties, while also capturing strength and motivation from those same feelings. I reframed my fragility to employ that energy productively, to keep driving myself forward. No matter how bleak I felt, I always tried to sustain my sense of fun.

Finding and stoking my embers got me through. I am sure your embers can help you too.

On the day after my crash, I learned that on top of the injuries they described to me on Sunday morning, a subsequent review of my scans had revealed a fractured left scapula (shoulder blade). I immediately tallied the numbers in my mind and saw the opportunity this new injury presented. I started joking that I had the 5:2 diet a bit wrong – instead of five days eating, two days fasting, I had five broken bones and two fractured vertebrae. For those poor visitors that gave the mildest glint of a smile at the first joke, I went on to tell them that I doubted my misinterpretation was going to catch on.

I didn't have the physical or emotional capability to reply to all the well-wishing text messages, but when I did respond it was with that same warped humour (copied and pasted). My Rio Tinto PACE team colleagues jumped on this, sending me a massive bucket of Lindt chocolates labelled: '5:2 diet: on doctor's orders'. Leigh wrote the kind covering note:

'Dear Mark,

We know you love a good yarn to tell, but really the lengths you will go! We are wishing you a speedy recovery. Hopefully a few choccies can sweeten up your post-physio recovery sessions.

From all your PACE workmates'

I wept again as I read it, overwhelmed and anxious. I had let them down. My input to the project would never have the influence it could have had. I worked with the organisation on a project-by-project contract basis; I might never get the chance to work with these great people again.

A few weeks later, once I regained an appetite for eating them, those chocolates were valuable as I gathered energy between intense physiotherapy efforts. As I savoured them, I reflected on the care with which they had been sent. Gratitude is a powerful ember.

Perhaps the best example of me stoking my humour and hope embers comes from a combination of events over my first few days. From the moment the paramedics reached me in that ditch, I was asked to give pain scores out of ten. Apparently I was initially replying with nines, and then after the treasured green whistle took the edge off the pain, I reassessed to eights. My cycling friend Mike later said that as he watched me respond, my strained expression and gasped breath suggested the pain was at least an 11.

During the days in acute care, almost every waking hour I was asked to give doctors and nurses that pain score out of ten. Between their visits, I was sore and confused. Every movement in bed was difficult. I would be exhausted by the prolonged effort to shuffle myself an inch up the bed to try and get into more comfortable positions, my right arm needing to pull or push me with all its current might to generate any movement, because my legs provided so little assistance and I didn't have any core strength capable of manoeuvring my torso. I was regularly processing what '50 per cent compression of your spinal cord' might mean for my future. Mentally I was extending that '50 per cent compression' to think, 'How do I get around with 50 per cent leg function?' so I genuinely felt my leg power was at best a five out of ten.

Perhaps six times each day, specialists, physiotherapists and nurses would come in. They would take off the uncomfortable square resting splint that my left foot had to be strapped into all day and night to protect its slim chance of recovery. Even lying down, my left foot was not strong enough to hold itself against gravity, and that 'foot drop' would cause additional ligament stretching. They would unplug and then remove the intermittent pneumatic compression device my calves wore all day – deep vein thrombosis being a risk for all bedridden patients – but in my case my lymphatic system was also struggling to operate and pump fluids away from my feet and ankles. They would roll back the tight compression socks such that my toes were exposed.

They would pull and push on my legs, feet and toes through a series of movements and angles, asking me to resist or push against their force. As they went through the series of movements for my whole leg, they would state a score: five for this, four for that. Those scores were stable from test to test and matched my expectation of 50 per cent. While it confirmed my legs were not functioning to their full power or capability, there was hope.

But for the movements relating to my feet and toes, the scores were only ones and zeros: ones are a twitch of movement and zeros reflect no movement at all. These scores were scary – next to hopeless. What did it mean for my mobility if I could not find a way to improve their capability? As I lay there on the first days, I didn't have the same appreciation of how important normal foot function is as I have today, but it was clear these scores were bad news.

I knew the low scores were because of my nerve damage, and between each visit I did everything I could to flex and move my toes, my feet – any small movement that I could manage, at least every hour, to sustain what I had and hopefully improve. I would lie there, mentally willing my toes towards me as I physically strained to generate twitches of movement. With each test I became increasingly anxious to hear improved scores, but any good news was trumped by a deterioration in the next test. It was disheartening to hear the scores for my foot dorsiflexion or big toe movement. Each zero or one was like having a nail hammered into me, deflating my hope that I might break free from my apparent damage and take those coveted steps towards mobility.

After a few days, I had the energy to ask for an explanation about this examination. I was told it was part of the American Spinal Cord Injury Association (ASIA) testing performed on spinal cord patients. I learned that the scale is out of five, not ten as I had assumed! Sure, this did not help the zeros and ones for my feet, but it brought enormous relief regarding the strength of my bigger leg muscles, some of which I now understood were being graded five out of five! I laughed. I allowed it to be a story of joy rather than bemoaning 'no-one told me the scale'. It stoked that ember of hope – suddenly there was a result that was not as bad as I had thought. Positivity is one of my embers.

Warmth grows from the faintest glow

Embers can be tiny. They can be faint. In a bushfire, the smallest spark can float on a breeze and start a new fire miles away.

Think back to the times you tended a fading fire and how your delicate, extended breaths spurred a flickering flame. Tiny embers and soft exhalations, building off each other from the gentlest beginnings. That smooth puff of passing air repeated over and over crackles the embers back to warmth, then gradually builds a blazing fire.

In his excellent book *The Psychology of Money*, Morgan Housel provides a series of examples to illustrate the compounding power of exponential growth. Morgan uses the cycles of the ice ages to show how immensely something can grow from a relatively small change. Variations in the Earth's orbit cause mildly cooler summers, which enable snow to accrue year to year. This build-up of snow reflects solar radiation, which perpetuates the cooling cycle.

The key message is that an accumulation of small increments create what appear to be step changes, or as Morgan puts it: 'You don't need tremendous force to create tremendous results'. All my tiny embers, rekindled by applying effort, were stoked by the gentlest interventions of love from others – this built the foundation for my recovery. The embers sparked my sense of self-worth.

Many of my embers were desperately faint, like my sense of identity. Some of my embers flickered, like my positivity. My family, friends and carers were so important in tending to these through the journey, keeping them slowly crackling their way back towards full roar. Every moment wasn't, and doesn't need to be, progressive, just as in the powerful shift of an ice age. It takes time and concerted effort.

My ability to recall treasured memories about who I was and what I loved was a powerful ember that never waned. An inner pilot light.

Our memories are embers

As a 21-year-old I had the privilege of representing the University of Western Australia on a field hockey tour around Germany, France and the Netherlands. It was just my second international adventure, the other being a family trip to New Zealand when I was ten. It was my trip of a lifetime, and I will never forget that amazing month: the beautiful scenery, exposure to history, playing an exhausting amount of hockey and, most of all, the incredible generosity of our many wonderful hosts.

Our final game was in Berlin, and that famous city delivered my most special memory, as my dear friend Benny and I were recounting the highlights from our prior day sightseeing to our wonderful host Tanya. We focused on our absorbing visit to Checkpoint Charlie, how it was confronting to walk where the wall divided Berlin north to south, to read the stories of fear and ill-fated escape attempts.

Tanya told us about her childhood in West Berlin and the complexity of seeing her grandparents, something Benny and I had always taken for granted. Tanya's grandparents lived in West Germany, and the family could travel to visit them by car, entering East Germany at Checkpoint Bravo, then travelling for about 200 km before reaching West Germany at Checkpoint Alpha. Each holiday they applied for permits to do this. If one was granted, they packed the car, drove to the checkpoint, and suffered invasive security checks. Some years they were allowed through, others they were turned away, disappointed and confused.

I will never fully comprehend what it was like for Tanya to grow up with such uncertainty, stranded in an island city, surrounded by a political regime with a totally different ideology. Growing up confined by barbed wire that had sprung up overnight, that became a wall, dividing your city for nearly 30 years.

Tanya personalised our experience of the Berlin Wall, changing it from just a historic TV story. Our appreciation of the personal implications of the wall came from Tanya sharing the impact on her family. Tanya told us how she had goosebumps, how she was shaking in excitement as she watched the wall being torn down. Four years later as she relived that day for us, she had goosebumps and she was trembling. And I had goosebumps beside her. A wall that was far removed from me suddenly had a story, a face, a heart.

Tanya, her family, her beautiful city of Berlin, all grew up tolerating uncertainty. They grew up seeing possibilities. They stoked embers of normality, such as visiting relatives. They grew up with demons: fear, oppression, isolation. And there were many angels: leaders pushing for reform and of course the effort of the people themselves, courageous East German protestors who risked so much to achieve change. Eventually that change came: Germany was reunified. A step change in the path to recovery. A new possible.

The destruction of the Berlin Wall is a strong symbol of embracing uncertainty, and how that enables the liberation of possibility. But what moved me most, what has stayed with me ever since that day, was Tanya's emotion as she spoke of the Berlin Wall. How it revealed a deep connection to her embers of normality – the effort to see her grandparents, the joy when she reached them, and the disappointment from those cancelled trips. Tanya never gave up seeking that joy and her family kept raking those embers. As I stoked mine. As you can ignite yours.

Embers are there, just dig among the ash

During a disruptive event, we can long for a return to 'normality'. My journey crystallised for me that this is the wrong focus – it is bound to fail. One of my long-term mentors, John, recently used the phrase 'another normal' relating to the phase of the COVID-19 pandemic that the US was navigating. I found it so apt – because every moment is another normal, to varying degrees. It is normal to have difficult or unpredictable days. Think of how often you have said, 'What a bizarre day', or heard it said. Life is dynamic. Life can be euphoric, and it can be challenging. Within that variation we find our depth of meaning.

Chasing the illusion of a past or new normal will only cause you disappointment. It reminds me of a leadership lesson I once received about not making false promises to yourself that it will get better. It taught me that I needed to grow accustomed to dealing with the ambiguity I faced, rather than longing for a sudden reduction in the complexity, especially with respect to the scarcity of resources or time.

In early 2021 I participated in a coaching call in which Cassandra Goodman, author of *Self-Fidelity*, was talking about the importance of finding your essence. It resonated with my concept of embers of normality, and as I listened to Cassie speak, I identified that my embers – my memories and events – were a crucial part of the essence of me. Her work captures the importance of connecting with who we are.

Instead of hunting for 'normality', find those elements of normal that connect to your character, your attitude, your friendships, the perspectives from your experiences. Your embers. Fuel those, because they are powerful for sustaining your identity and purpose. These elements of your essence help you move and embrace the uncertainty of what is ahead. They are the embers of normality that enable you to persevere and succeed as you move forward, as you face your fears and uncertainties.

Even within the most unsettling change, it's possible to seek out embers of normality. These are the embers that help you remain connected with your identity, even in the most challenging times.

You must nurture these embers that light your life – these things that make you tick, give you joy, provide purpose.

If helplessness is descending, rekindle your embers. Picture yourself raking them up – like stoking a fire. Feel their warmth on your cheeks and the contentment they bring to your heart. Use the strength of these feelings to help you connect to your deepest identity, your most treasured feelings. It will make you stronger, help you to believe and to persevere.

Let your embers – your sense of meaning – drive you towards your exceptional outcome.

Become a fraction stronger

- What embers can you identify for yourself? What are the things that connect you most strongly to your identity?
- What memories do you have that make you feel warm inside?
- What are some quotes or sayings that resonate deeply with you?
- Can you think of some compliments that have been paid to you recently that have filled you with pride?
- How might you remind yourself of your embers? Can you write them down and display them somewhere prominent, so you can find strength in them every day?

Chapter 5

Exploring pathways

'Don't be satisfied with stories, how things have gone
with others, unfold your own myth.'
– Rūmī

I suspect I was born curious. But I have no doubt that my parents' efforts to expose me and my brother Peter to different interests engaged and extended that natural tendency. Arts, drama, hiking, music, road trips and sport, to name a few. When I was ten years old, we caravanned our way around Australia for nearly six months. Despite doing almost no schoolwork for a semester, my subsequent reports show the adventure expanded my ability to learn. I am sure this natural and nurtured inclination to be open-minded and explore helped my recovery journey.

Experiences from my corporate career also influenced who I am and how I tackled my predicament. I could recall lessons and past successes in dealing with change, navigating ambiguity, overcoming anxiety and pursuing improvement. But it was the skills and experience I had accumulated in negotiation that were the most influential.

I am certain those acquired skills that helped me can benefit you – practical skills such as testing assumptions, asking questions, listening for signals of flexibility and exploring for possibility. This is what I did when I heard the specialist's words 'Every spinal cord injury is unique' and extrapolated it into 'Every recovery can be unique'. I intended to explore that possibility with all my spirit.

Seeking pathways

It wasn't enough to just persuade myself that there was hope. I needed to seek pathways to strengthen that hope. The pathways didn't need to be firm, just possible. But I also needed to prepare myself for shortfall against my hopes. I needed to find and reinforce the benefits to me, even if I fell short of my goals.

One of my first actions was to challenge my assumptions around what success looked like. I knew that testing assumptions is an important technique to help keep an open mind and avoid constraining outcomes.

I absolutely wanted success to look like full recovery, but that was not in my control. I could only contribute to that likelihood with sustained focus and effort. So, I challenged myself to think about how I could feel successful even if I fell short of my goals. This was important, because only by identifying what I really wanted would I generate sustainable drivers that could motivate me through the ups and downs of recovery. Defining success poorly would constrain my outcomes.

As I pondered how to do this, I concluded that I really had two 'must achieve' outcomes:

1. to improve as much as I possibly could
2. to apply the most positive attitude I could towards improving.

The latter enabled the former and provided sustainable motivation. No matter what happened in terms of physical improvement, through my attitude I could set a good example for my children and for others – as Lucy and so many others had set great examples before me. This included exploring all possible pathways for achieving better outcomes.

I applied the trait of keeping an open mind. Or, as my friend and negotiation mentor Mark would say, I used the 'open-door technique'. This is where you open the door to what might be possible by providing and inviting information. Hypothesise both in your thinking and your interactions: 'Just suppose' this was the case, what might I be able to achieve? Using this technique, we can uncover potential pathways that warrant exploration. It promotes curiosity.

The curiosity, endeavour and persistence of the Wright brothers pioneered flight, so it is not surprising Orville is quoted as saying, 'If we all worked on the assumption that what is accepted as true is really true, there would be little hope of advance'.

That is exactly the attitude I took forward from that first day – how do I explore what might be possible? How can I find flexibility in what I have heard to direct my effort and foster my belief? How do I discover pathways that provide greater scope, and therefore more hope, of achieving better outcomes?

It started when I decided to extrapolate the curve of possible outcomes on that first morning – beyond the prognosis and towards full recovery. *Under what circumstances might the outcomes that I so desperately want be possible? What do I need to believe for that to be achievable? How do I concentrate my actions to enhance my prospects of regaining identity and independence? How do I address my needs and worries?*

People negotiate based on their needs and worries. Those negotiations are driven by 'must achieve' (or 'must avoid') elements and 'would like to achieve' (or avoid) elements. That initial doctors' briefing had placed me in a negotiation with myself. *How will I respond?*

How can I make this work? What information do I have? What information do I need? What are my options? What are the benefits of giving this my best shot, even if I fail?

I was driven by a need to physically recover. Mobility had been central to my life so far, and was important to how I pictured my future life. I was worried about being a burden to my family – I did not want to fathom a life without my physical independence, where they were impacted in an ongoing way.

I can't help but feel self-conscious when I reflect on those emotions, because they now feel overblown. Many people get through tougher things than I had to endure. Some people are confronted with news so devastating there is almost no hope. Some people give their all but can't change the trajectory of their recovery. They find ways to deal with those lasting impacts, proving themselves to be inspirational for how they coped and continue to cope with their setbacks – how they discover and share new meaning.

Provided my operation was successful, I understood that there was hope of attaining a reasonable level of recovery. The potential of my improvement would be a function of the extent of the nerve damage and my application. Even with this upside, the news was shattering. It caused me to process images of myself in a wheelchair – able to stand and step a few metres but needing ongoing help from my family to get the wheelchair in and out of the car. Instead of being the proud, strong father dashing from activity to activity, interacting with his beautiful children, cheering their achievements, I would be an invalid slowing them down, rendering many aspects of our lives more difficult. On top of this diffusion of family identity, activities that I treasured were potentially gone forever. Like the feeling of squeaky beach sand between my toes and the sensory liberation of swimming in the ocean. The adrenalin of pushing myself for long hours as I cooked up a delicious, complex, three-course dinner party for 12. Life would be less flexible; my passion for travel would be restricted.

With time and effort, I have recaptured much of this identity that seemed to be leaking away from me on that first day. I appreciate I benefited from circumstantial good fortune. Many don't have all the advantages that helped me – access to a first-class public health system, private health cover, accumulated wealth to buffer the financial impacts of trauma, an extensive support network. But I assure you, people who don't have my tailwinds find a way to succeed too. Acknowledging that so many people have it tougher but still apply themselves, still achieve amazing things, really helped me. And it may help you too.

Never die wondering

This process of negotiating with myself – of internalising my needs – made me think of an ember: the humour, hope and conviction I associate with the idiom 'Never die wondering'. This had become a key phrase during my role as Rio Tinto's Chief Negotiator Iron Ore Pricing. Generating substantial benefit for the Australian economy, the role required all the relationship, teamwork and negotiating skills I had gathered to that point of my career. I associate the phrase 'Never die wondering' with so many important memories: testing boundaries, achieving high-quality results in adverse conditions and, most of all, balancing that with fun thanks to fabulous team camaraderie.

To perform consistently under pressure in our negotiations, our team started using a series of phrases to remind us of key negotiation behaviours, steps and skills. The most memorable of these phrases related to our cue to ask questions – internally and externally – and test assumptions. This is important because untested assumptions preclude you from discovering additional information, thereby constraining possibility.

When I commenced in that role, Peter, a friend who led our Shanghai office, would beamingly smile and quip 'Never die wondering' if I grumbled about the unwavering ability of our Chinese customers to ask for improved terms, no matter how optimistic in the context of their agreed contractual obligations. These requests were normally triggered by a change in market conditions to their favour.

We adopted 'Never die wondering' to remind us of the value of exploring and testing assumptions through questions. The phrase prompted us to listen and watch carefully, to be courageous, to test and overcome constraints.

During my recovery, I adopted 'Never die wondering' to remind me to listen carefully to the medical experts, *and* to explore what else might be possible. I used 'Never die wondering' to remind me to try hard, to embrace uncertainty and to visualise my best possible outcome. It reminded me to make hypotheses about what might be achievable, and figure out what I needed to do to support that; to always keep an open mind about my situation and how to adapt to new information, good or bad; and to explore for opportunity. It reminded me to sustain a sense of fun, wherever possible. It still does all those things today.

Keep your pathways open

The American novelist Virginia Woolf reminds us to broaden our perspectives with her expression, 'There is no gate, no lock, no bolt that you can set upon the freedom of my mind'.

In my first few days and weeks of recovery, I encouraged myself to keep an open mind about whether the impacts of my nerve damage might pass. My foot and toe movement losses impacted both feet, but they were worse on the left side, which still gave zeros and ones on that ASIA test versus ones and twos on the right side. My fractured scapula, ribs and wrist were all left side, and the bruising was far worse to my left side. I hoped that as that bruising subsided, especially in my lower back, my sensory feedback might improve. I didn't set any expectations; I just explored the possibility. And I did everything I could to keep moving as much as possible, especially whatever small foot movements I could muster, as it supported all the possible outcomes I was targeting.

In every meeting with my specialists, I'd explore my prospects with questions, aiming to build up a picture of the array of possible outcomes and the pathways that might lead me towards recovery. The physiotherapists helped me contextualise what I was feeling, what was ahead and how I might achieve better outcomes, especially during my short daily walks leaning on a rollator – a rolling walking frame. The frame almost wraps around you, with padded rests for your forearms and vertical hand grips that your clasp onto.

In all those discussions, I established a strong association between my longer-term prospects and achieving early gains. That knowledge was the fuel to sustain my perseverance through my initial challenges. It also meant some of our early decisions were crucial.

By the end of my first week in hospital, one of our most important decisions started to take shape – what next after I was discharged from acute care? It was unclear how long I would require hospitalisation, but it was certainly weeks and possibly months. The hospital proposed to transfer me to their nearby Geriatric and Rehabilitation Unit (GARU), but Lucy pushed back hard. She encouraged and helped me to explore what else might be possible. I am thankful Lucy stepped in, because without her drive it would have been easy to acquiesce with what the hospital – the Royal Brisbane and Women's Hospital (RBWH) – wanted. I was shaken, clinging for hope and forming trust in the RBWH physiotherapists. Consistency with their treatment was appealing – it provided comfort. There are often many roads to success, but in this case, we made a crucial intervention to take a harder step at the time, delivering later benefit.

As I would learn when I started my outpatient check-ups, RBWH is an inconvenient hospital to access both from a parking and traffic congestion perspective. Even though we live quite close to Brisbane's CBD, from our home it was at best a 40-minute effort by the time Lucy and kids arrived bedside, and in peak traffic a lot longer than that. As well as juggling her busy full-time job and dealing with phone calls about my welfare, Lucy was keeping life on the rails for our kids, who were (then) Year 12, Year 11 and Year 7 students who all had extra-curricular activities on top of their school lives. Fortunately, as is customary around us, the school community was generously creating meal rosters and offering other assistance.

A concerted effort led to me getting admitted to Princess Alexandra Hospital (PAH) GARU. PAH is the location of Queensland's Spinal Injuries Unit, so that team could readily check in on my progress, and the physiotherapists who treated me in the GARU all had experience treating spinal injuries. Perhaps more importantly, this facility was less than ten minutes from our home, so it was much more accessible for family and friends. This convenience proved immensely valuable to me as their visits were vital to my mindset, rekindling embers and providing timely support.

This important outcome is an example of the value of clearly explaining your needs and exploring under which circumstances they might be possible. We were specific in what we wanted and why, which is a distinguishing feature of successful proposals in any negotiation.

I was transferred by ambulance over to PAH on my 12th day of recovery. I amused myself by sending the cycling chat group a picture of myself smiling away with text along the lines of 'A little happier than my last ride in an ambulance'. Not long after induction I was introduced to my new physio, Lucy, who assessed my capacity (safety) for independent movement. I was surprised and thrilled when she cleared me to move about the ward on my own rollator! It even got a tag with my name on it.

To put this in context, in RBWH Acute Care I'd had one daily walk on the rollator for up to ten minutes, which was an exhausting process.

A physio would arrive, unplug me from my various attachments, sit me up, put on my socks (I was unable to reach my feet), position the hard plastic ankle foot orthosis (AFO) that my left leg needed, as I was unable to lift my foot, then put on my shoes, before strapping the AFO to my leg. Getting the AFO both into my left shoe and onto my leg was a bit of a knack we had to master. It took enormous energy while also making me feel completely helpless in the process.

Once we were ready, another physio would be located and off I'd lurch, with a physio on each side for safety. It was tough and exhausting, but I was moving forward. I'd pushed myself as hard as I could on each walk. After a week I'd improved enough that I could walk on the rollator with just one person assisting me, which also meant I could use the rollator to reach the bathroom to shower myself (sitting in a chair) or to get to the chair in my room. I'd call a nurse, who would do all that same preparatory work for me to get up, then they'd help get me to the bathroom or the chair. I would sit in the chair for as long as I could each day. It hurt and fatigued me more than lying in bed, but I was convinced that sitting up was a valuable progression, helping my mindset, muscles and lungs.

I had assumed I would have the same movement limitations at PAH, so you can imagine my joy when physio Lucy liberated me! It opened opportunities for me to test and extend my movement capabilities, even if it was scary getting myself from bed to the rollator at times, and especially from the rollator to the dining room chairs. Pushing myself to the edge of my capabilities meant I was testing constraints; I was opening pathways.

Having my own rollator was liberating, but I was expected to wear shoes and the AFO. I was still dependent on getting help to put these on, which was a frustrating constraint. Instead, I chose independence. Whenever I could, I walked around the ward barefoot, as I didn't have the toe strength to keep thongs (flip flops) on my feet and I wanted to avoid the AFO.

It took a bit over a week in the PAH before I put my shoes and AFO on without help for the first time. While this eliminated the constraint of waiting for help, mainly I was driven by pride – to achieve another mini milestone towards recovery. It was almost ten minutes of exhausting effort, sweating profusely and my legs jagging about wildly due to my inability to control them under strain. But I did it. I was proud of my determination. Another pathway opened.

Wearing the AFO felt horrible. Imagine having a piece of hard, cheap plastic sitting under your foot from just behind your big toe, wrapping around the edge of your foot and heel, then running up the back of your leg to the top of your calf. It is designed to hold the foot in a fixed position, so you can still walk if you have lost the ability to control your foot, as I had.

To the spinal specialists, the AFO was required because of my physical deficiencies, to stop me tripping on my left foot, and to reduce circumvention of my left leg: swinging the foot outwards given I couldn't lift it up. To me the AFO represented long-term immobility. It was a constraint that I wanted to test and remove. I felt that wearing it reduced my slim chances of full recovery, because the foot was fixed into position by the AFO. If I allowed myself to rely on the AFO, then my foot would get weaker, and I might lose that use forever. I wanted to make all of me stronger, fraction by fraction.

In hospital, and for at least six months after discharge, all the specialists I met told me I would wear an AFO for the rest of my life – albeit a customised, lightweight carbon-fibre one. I didn't want to accept that outcome, and each time AFOs were discussed, it boosted my resolve to apply effort to improve, to find another way. Even just seeing that AFO fuelled me. I disliked looking at it or touching it because it was a visual symbol of my loss of movement, my loss of identity. If I couldn't step away from using the AFO, I had – at least partially – failed.

When the specialists told me that my barefoot walking had to stop, that I had to wear the AFO, I negotiated. We reached agreement that I would wear it for some parts of my twice-daily rehabilitation program and if I left the ward, because there were more trip hazards in the outside world. This agreement meant we spent time protecting and developing my leg swing (AFO on) and protecting my foot strength (AFO off). It also meant more of my limited energy was spent on focused recovery versus the physical complexity of putting on shoes!

A step change

Three weeks into my PAH GARU stay, I received an intervention that I am sure changed the trajectory of my recovery. Physio Lucy jumped on an opportunity to secure a session for me with the head physiotherapist, Leanne, who had signalled a willingness to work with additional patients at their weekly review meeting.

By that stage, I was completely fed up with hospital and I desperately wanted to get home. We tentatively planned I would discharge at the end of the next week, but we didn't have an effective rehabilitation plan for how I would continue to find the level of treatment I required after discharge. Then Leanne changed my plans. She caused me to rethink what might be possible.

Leanne was late to that first session. I'd been waiting with anticipation, and I remember thinking that I was going to miss out. It was quite the reverse, as Leanne worked through her lunch hour with me, when the gym was typically shut to patients. Leanne was small, fit and strong. She was the epitome of no-nonsense – every action was committed to helping me achieve better results.

That first session was confronting. I recall one of the first things Leanne asked me to do was take my shirt off, so that she was able to see just how many of my muscles I had to recruit to do simple activities like standing. She sat me down on a Bobath table (a physiotherapy treatment table) and asked me to perform movements such as tapping my toes off the floor. As she walked around me, she was able to identify and explain how I was recruiting almost every working muscle, all the way up my body, to do these tasks, as my body was compensating for its injury-related deficiencies. With all that applied effort, I could lift the front of my left foot 1 cm and the right foot perhaps 3 cm. And my fatigue number for those movements was low – I could manage about ten of these toe lifts on the right, and perhaps five on the left, before no strength remained and the exercise could no longer be repeated. And remember, for the preceding month at nearly every opportunity I had been wriggling, flexing, straining and tapping these feet and toes to sustain strength and try to stimulate any potential recovery.

Leanne instructed me to stand with my hips against a Bobath table, standing with legs straight, feet at almost shoulder width. She pivoted me at the waist so that my upper body was perpendicular to my legs, my face prone on the table. The Bobath table was needed as Leanne would electronically fine tune the height so that I was hinged in exactly the right position. She then taught me how to do small pelvic tilting movements, trying to awaken the small core muscles that were locked in some protective shield around my damage core. She would guide these movements – firstly, by helping me make them at all, then by encouraging the range of movement to be slightly extended.

Each session we would do this, or a similar exercise in which I stood against the wall and pelvic tilted, trying to re-establish my capability to engage and feel these muscles again. Sometimes Leanne would work other specific areas, such as stimulating my heel and foot. All these actions were carefully targeted, trying to awaken my neurological pathways.

These steps were part of coaching me in the dynamics of walking. Because of my sensory disruption, my body had lost all sense of what to do.

Together Leanne and I would stand at the end of my little 'runway' in the gym, Leanne wrapping one arm around my shoulders and the other arm applying bracing pressure at my waist, supporting the upper half of my body. Without that support I had insufficient balance and strength to hold myself up.

I was instructed to walk as fast as I could. As we walked in unison, I tried to concentrate on those specific neural pathways she had just stimulated – such as generating a heel strike. Leanne was physically directing my body to wake up nerve pathways, to reconnect. It was scary, exhilarating, demoralising, inspiring. I had limited control of my legs, and no control of my feet. They would smash into the ground as we walked as fast as I could: slap, slap, slap.

I ended up having five sessions with Leanne. At each session, Leanne would target one or two specific muscle areas for manipulation to stimulate the neural pathways disrupted by my spinal cord damage, before we did our conjoined walking to finish each session. It felt like quite the grandstand finish to me, because of the way the treatment built up to those six or so laps down our seven-metre-long runway. Typically, a few other physios or gym staff would be there watching, encouraging my effort and progression as I marched at the edge of control, relying on Leanne to keep me upright and safe. Our intertwined position, and the slapping noise from feet on the floor, meant it provided an engaging spectacle.

Leanne opened pathways. She showed me how to tackle my constraints. And she gave me reason to retest some assumptions. In those first days post-accident I had hoped my apparent nerve damage was only temporary. But as time ground on, I learned just how slow and difficult progress was. I was starting to accept that the 12 mm piece of vertebra may have indeed severed my spinal cord, and my hopes.

Leanne provided a different perspective on my damage than I had received from the specialists. She likened my body to a car that had violently crashed, where the wiring of that car had been loosened and connections shaken free from their rightful place at the time of impact. Fortunately, our bodies are smart cars. There was hope of getting the car wiring working again, but I needed to stimulate the pathways to reconnect that wiring, or relearn how to use the connections that were left. It provided hope versus the alternative hypothesis – that the clean cut in my spinal cord meant the non-working parts of my body were impacted forever.

I don't think Leanne is particularly sentimental. She was just doing her job. But those sessions changed my outcomes. They wouldn't have happened without physio Lucy hearing Leanne's signal of flexibility to treat somebody and exploring it. Or without my flexibility to adapt my plans and stay in hospital for longer when I desperately wanted to leave.

Leanne's intervention provided a vital step change to my progression. It liberated possibilities about the extent I might recover. Leanne's actions and perspectives brightened my belief about the outcomes I might achieve. And for those pathways that she and physio Lucy opened up for me, I will be eternally grateful.

In much the same way as Leanne and Lucy opened pathways for me, Karni Liddell's parents, who we met in chapter 3, opened the door to possibility by testing the boundaries of what they had heard. They did it in a balanced way, focusing on lower-impact activities and utilising home-made exercise equipment that helped Karni gradually develop strength. They explored and trialled a wide range of activities to see what worked. Their effort to open her world to new possibilities inspired me to see greater possibility nearly 40 years later. Such is the power of opening pathways.

When you are amid significant change or uncertainty, it is important to be careful not to constrain yourself with assumptions. Be curious and encourage yourself to keep opening the door to what else might be possible.

There is often so much value and potential that you can't see or predict. Only by opening new pathways do these opportunities become visible. Be alert; listen and watch for these opportunities, and be flexible in your approach so that you can adapt to them.

The world is full of possibility if we choose to explore it.

Just suppose. Open the door.

Become a fraction stronger

- Are you afraid to negotiate – to ask questions and explore possibilities?
- What areas of your life are you viewing at face value, rather than digging deeper to explore what could be?
- Thinking of an issue or situation you're currently experiencing, what other options could you possibly explore?
- Do you know someone who is always pushing the boundaries, living life on their own terms? What inspires you about that way of living?
- What assumptions have you made about the issue you are facing, your role in life or your relationships? How might you explore or challenge these?
- Just suppose you were able to solve the problem you are facing. What might you be able to achieve?
- What does the phrase 'Never die wondering' mean to you?

Part II

ANG-ELS

Precious progress, rekindled hope,
Fragments of new belief.
The purity of kindness, a flicker inside us,
A minute of light-hearted relief.
A visit, a memory, a smile or a thought.
Your angels arrive, with their priceless support.

A decision to own, a warmer tone,
Peace, with a book or a friend.
A new goal set, a milestone met,
Or simply, a night on the mend.
Some guidance, a vision, the taste of fresh food.
Angels within and around, boosting our mood.

Embrace those angels, their timeless relief,
Nurture love, cherish kindness and foster belief.
Resolute effort and heartfelt care,
Your secret wings, to soar anywhere.

In January 2013, Cameron Bloom, his wife Sam and their three young boys set off for a dream holiday in Thailand. Realising that Phuket wasn't their style, they drove north until they found somewhere quieter. They settled on a small, no-frills hotel on an empty beach. Serenity.

They enjoyed a perfect first morning before tragedy struck. As the family were exploring the hotel's observation deck, Sam leant against a railing, which gave way. She fell six metres onto the blue concrete tiles below.

Can you imagine the devastation of the boys, looking down on their mother, smashed and broken below? The dread Cam must have felt, racing to be with Sam, crying for help? The fear they faced, waiting for the ambulance – fear that was sustained for more than four agonising hours as they sped towards the nearest hospital capable of treating Sam? The uncertainty of the three-day wait until Sam was strong enough to be operated on? The nerve-racking hours during that life-saving surgery?

Cam and the boys stayed by her side. Angels willing her on, wishing her strength. Then Sam's mum was beside her too, having flown from Australia with all possible urgency. As you would. As a mum, as an angel. Then her best friend Bron arrived, too.

Sam was in excruciating pain for weeks. Her injuries were extensive and incredibly severe. She could have passed. But she fought on. She lived. Cam stayed by her side.

After three weeks Sam was stable enough to be medically escorted to Australia. Paramedics met her flight on arrival. She was taken to Royal North Shore Hospital, where Sam learned the awful truth that her spinal cord damage was permanent. She was paralysed from the chest down. She would never stand or walk again. Hearing that news was like reliving the gut-wrenching helplessness of plummeting from that observation deck.

The impact was devastating. It shattered Sam's identity. It flattened all sense of hope.

Sam spent six months hospitalised in Sydney, roughly half in a spinal rehabilitation unit. There were many difficult and confronting moments. Her angels kept coming: family, friends and all the amazing carers who had her back, providing her with intense care during her recovery. Helping her build those basic skills she would need to transfer to life at home. And Sam craved to get home.

And then Sam came home. She describes this as the worst day of her life because it was the moment when the reality of her physical condition struck her. Her loss of independence. Her loss of identity.

Cam and all Sam's other angels were steadfast. They did everything they could to support Sam. But life was difficult on so many levels.

Then, out of the blue, a new angel arrived. A unique one. Penguin – a magpie blown out of a nest, injured. The family adopted Penguin, and caring for that bird changed Sam's perspective. It prompted the bestselling book-turned-movie *Penguin Bloom* and Sam's beautiful story *Heartache and Birdsong*. Slowly the dark cloud over Sam's life started to lift.

Sam and Penguin formed a special connection. With a damaged wing and a wobbly head, Penguin was fragile and needed care. This awakened Sam's instincts, rekindled her identity.

> 'To this day I remain astonished that two shiny eyes and a few grams of fluff could rescue me from bitter oblivion and help save my family, but that is exactly what happened.'

Penguin changed Sam's perspective. She gave Sam's life focus and a new connection with her family. Sam started to believe that if Penguin could mend, she could too. When Penguin finally flew, Sam's heart soared. Watching Penguin fly motivated Sam to commit to her own recovery: 'Penguin was living proof that – with enough love, support and hard work – hope can become reality.'

Our angels emerge in many forms, and just when we need them. Sam found a kindred spirit in Penguin. There were many other angels too, including Cam and the boys, and Sam's supportive family, friends and carers. And finally, Sam's own effort and belief, which found new wings with the help of this magical little magpie.

I know from my own journey that angels are stronger and more diverse than I ever imagined. They encouraged me when I was progressing, and they picked me up when I was fragile. I could literally write hundreds of stories covering the powerful little acts that enabled me to persevere, that guided me, that replenished my spirit. I could never have achieved the same outcomes without them, and I will be forever grateful for their influence on my recovery.

External help was important, but I was also driven by my internal angels. I fostered my own attitude, effort and imagination. The influence of these powerful inner angels was totally within my control.

In my darkest moments I reached for these angels of my past and my imagination. I conjured up all the memories and inspiration that I could, by visualising other people's successes. I thought about how I might emulate just a fraction of their efforts and outcomes. In each tough moment I revisited these thoughts, extended by memories of the new successes I had accumulated in my journey so far. I built resolve so that I could persevere.

You can do this too. These first thoughts just need to be directional – a few sparks of belief. And then you extend and strengthen your own belief from those sparks.

Angels move you. Angels change your perspective. Angels will help you soar again, if you welcome and embrace their care.

Chapter 6

Reaching out and in

'Even the smallest kindness shall not be forgotten.'
– Japanese proverb

Have you ever woken from major surgery? Woozy, hungry, dependent. I think the care you require in those first hours crystallises an incredible bond between yourself and those first faces around you. I can still sense the kindness radiated by the nurse who looked after me during my first night in acute care, doing her job with efficiency and compassion. Checking on me hourly, when I was at my weakest, my most vulnerable and defeated. (Apparently, I was also delirious and attempting to be funny.) Even as time fades her face and causes her name to evade me, the magnitude of gratitude that I feel towards her stands resolute.

Lucy was there, too, exhausted after what must have been a horrific day. Having her peace disrupted by a phone call, rushing to the hospital uncertain of what would confront her. Finding me in a bad way, but with no inkling it could be as severe as that shocking news we'd receive a couple of hours later. Words that almost triggered her to faint, even though she has as much fortitude as anyone I know.

A day spent racing back and forth between hospital and keeping our home running. Waiting for news of operating success. Feeding me yoghurt after midnight as I slurred my way back into the conscious world, then returning home to sleep and juggle her working week. Posting a photo to Instagram of me looking drained post-surgery: 'Not the Sunday we all expected...'

How could I ever adequately express my gratitude to all those angels who reached out to me in those tough days, weeks and months? The visits, messages, flowers and chocolates. Our old neighbour, Margaret, arriving with the most beautiful fruit salad I can remember eating. Clearly it was just what my body was seeking at that point – something fresh and revitalising. The skill and care of so many specialists, nurses, social workers and others.

Embracing the care gravitating towards me was enormously influential to my recovery. People doing their jobs, people investing time and effort to cheer me in hospital or sending gifts. Their care distracted my attention, luring me from improvident dwelling: *why did the bike stop cornering?* They were the friendly shore that made sure any wallowing in self-pity was restricted to the shallows.

I am certain that I was aided in finding the strength of my own spirit by these beautiful spirits around me. They tended my embers; they stoked my resolve. Their visits and care helped me reach in and gather up all my inner strength. They sparked me to marshal all my positive sentiment about who I was, about what I had experienced and achieved before, how I might get through this.

Even when so much of me felt broken, my spirit was capable of being nurtured. I think Lucy's words as she posted a photo of me transferring from RBWH to PAH sum it up perfectly: 'Thank you for all the kind words and support we have received. It certainly helps to keep a smile on Mark's face.'

I could find moments to smile because I had angels supporting me. I had embers that were being rekindled. I had reason. I had hope.

Breaching the help threshold

During my thirties I had to work through a few anxiety issues, caused by an accumulation of work and financial pressures. They stemmed from being a young father with high expectations of how I wanted to provide for my family. I fretted that if I didn't succeed in my roles, that would destabilise the home finances and put undue pressure on Lucy. My thoughts were due to a loss of perspective, as can happen when something triggers our deeper emotions. The episodes gave me invaluable experience in how hard it can be seeking help, but more importantly, in how beneficial seeking and accepting help can be. If I can share one key message: it is never too early or too late to reach out.

In 2005 Debra Rickwood and colleagues at the University of Wollongong researched why people, especially young men, resist asking for help when they need it. Their agenda was to identify factors that inhibit or encourage people to reach out for help. While the research focused on young people experiencing psychological distress, I believe it may apply more broadly because of the consistency of their findings with my lived experience. My recovery was the confluence of support from others and my self-reflection – the powerful convergence of 'out' with 'in'.

The researchers defined help-seeking as 'the process of actively seeking out and utilising social relationships, either formal or informal, to help with personal problems'. They noted that seeking help is an intensely personal experience, and identified a range of important enablers, including:

- access to established and trusted support pathways or relationships
- positive experiences with, and therefore positive attitude towards, the benefits of support

- encouragement from family, friends or social network
- asking for a friend – young people, in particular, are more likely to seek help for their friends than themselves.

I was able to access trusted support pathways. I could draw on existing positive experiences that gave me the courage to reach out for help. And I was fortunate to receive an enormous breadth of encouragement.

Our lives are constantly changing. Every day we deal with disruptions; it is just the extent of the disruption that varies. There are infinite little self-adjustments that we can make, such as shifting our mood or energy, that help us deal with these disruptions. Just like the suspension of a car helps the car weather bumps in the road.

By improving our awareness of how these adjustments help us deal with change, we build resilience. We enhance our understanding of how to recognise and work through our problems. We gather trust in our available support and the embers of experience about how we access, cope with and benefit from that support.

By elevating our consciousness of these experiences, of how we reach in for self-awareness and reach out for support, we build trust in our support systems and develop the courage to ask for help when we need it. We make ourselves a fraction stronger.

Reach for your hopes

The moment when you are tackling uncertainty is not the moment for dwelling in preciousness or pride. I was chasing an improbable outcome, and I needed all the help I could uncover. Putting aside my ego and sharing my fragilities was often difficult, but I was desperate and kept challenging myself to do so.

Lucy and I reached out beyond our direct network, seeking favours. We asked people we trusted to delve into their own networks to obtain advice for us to consider: opinions that enabled us to better understand my treatment options, to evaluate them and plan our next steps. The counsel we received, particularly via several of Lucy's friends, was integral to my recovery. The crucial decision to transfer me to PAH GARU could not have been made with the same confidence, if at all, without their help and reassurance.

The move to PAH proved to be an important one for many reasons, including that I ended up requiring seven weeks of in-hospital care. I was hoping for two! I desperately wanted to end the inconvenience of hospital (for me and my visitors) and be home contributing to the family. I wanted to resume the activities I loved, such as being involved in my children's sport and other endeavours. I was so determined to do my best, to improve, to get home.

As soon as I was told that I would transfer to PAH, my heart lit up with a hope. PAH was just ten minutes' drive from the ground where my eldest boy, Luke, would play his final AFL game for his school that Friday night. Just suppose there was a way I could get there.

It was more than an outing. It was a milestone that was important to my mindset, my identity.

I started reaching out, exploring. First, I asked my main RBWH physiotherapist, Andy, his opinion on the possibility, and how I might go about making my case. Andy explained that I'd need medical approval, and that the resident doctor would not grant that unless both physiotherapy and occupational therapy approved. I reached for, and Andy provided, guidance on how I might tackle those discussions. I would need to demonstrate that we could overcome and manage certain physical impediments for the hospital to approve.

I contacted one of my close friends, Steve. His son also played for the school AFL team, so he would be there. He and his wife are nurses. 'Can you help me get there, and make sure I am monitored while I am there?' I knew if I wanted the hospital to support my temporary release, I needed to provide the doctors with confidence I would be safe.

Armed with how I was going to manage the risks – which was a 'must achieve' for the hospital to address in any discussion – I was in a much better position to start the negotiation about how to get out. I explained the situation to physio Lucy, who arranged for an occupational therapist to coach me and check that I could safely manage the transitions from my wheelchair to the car and back out again. I was wheeled down to the occupational therapy (OT) centre, where they have a cutaway car for this purpose. It took most of my strength, but I could do it.

I was happy when I passed the test, and even happier when Madi, the lovely doctor who would sign off on my excursion, came by to ask for more information about the outing and why it was important. At the end of our discussion, she confirmed she would allow my release for about two hours on that Friday evening. I was so delighted and uplifted. Reflecting on what this meant to me still invokes strong emotions two and a half years later.

It felt wonderful and awful as I was wheeled to the footy ground in a wheelchair. It was a perfect evening and a pleasure to be outside. The only other fresh air I had enjoyed in the two weeks since the accident was the few seconds as they rolled me into an ambulance during the transfer to PAH.

Being out in the world inflamed the rawness of my loss. I felt conspicuous being so weak and vulnerable, with a catheter drain strapped to my leg. I felt shame about being so badly injured. Seeing friends from our school community 'as they were' reinforced the uncertainty of 'where I was' and what lay ahead. It was a struggle to mask my fragility whenever someone spoke to me for more than a sentence or two.

I was desperate to stand up for at least a minute to demonstrate – to myself, to others – that I could. To show my resolve. Steve wheeled me in front of a barrier, enabling me to use that rail as support to lean on, as my legs weren't strong enough to hold me by themselves.

Pushing myself upright from the wheelchair consumed a lot of energy. Standing made my back ache, my legs twitch and my feet swell. But the achievement energised me. I was reaching out towards my identity, with the help of my angels.

It was both a liberation and a necessity to be there. A timely intervention in my soul-sapping battle, allowing me to reconnect with aspects of life that I loved. To proudly cheer my son, surrounded by family and friends. To move forward.

It was a proclamation of intent.

The power of reaching out

A bonus reason to be at the game was Brian. I wanted to show him I was progressing.

Brian coached Luke in the AFL team and the school cross-country team. I knew him a little, but not well. The week before, while I had still been at RBWH, I was startled when he turned up in hospital with James Kerr's book *Legacy*, in which I later discovered his handwritten note, which brought me to tears. At the centre of his stirring inscription was a reference to a St Augustine quote: 'Lay first the foundation of humility… the higher the structure is to be, the deeper must be the foundation.'

Brian wrote that I had a deep foundation already; I needed to connect with it to build on it. And with humility I could rise again.

Brian illustrated the power you can create by reaching out to share something deeply personal from within when he chose to invest his precious weekend in coming to see me and share his story. Practising humility – as Brian did – enabled me to embrace the care that was offered and build an exceptional recovery.

Brian grew up with asthma, but he didn't let it hold him back. He loved cross-country running. He took up swimming understanding it was good for his lungs, based on advice he received from John, a sports physician and close family friend. Encouraged by his dad, Brian joined a surf club to extend that passion for the water. He discovered a love of surfboats. He felt free being in or on the water.

As part of his training in surfboat rowing, Brian cycled three days per week with two buddies.

Brian decided to enter a cycling race to test his cycling at a competitive level. He won his debut race but was disqualified by the officials due to the state of his helmet. If he wanted to compete, it needed to be upgraded. That afternoon he bought a new helmet that met the strict criteria so he could be eligible for future events.

The next week, Brian and his cycling buddies had cancelled their Friday morning ride, but Brian woke on autopilot. He decided to cycle solo. As he rode, the driver of a white Holden Commodore abused and challenged him at a set of traffic lights. The confrontation attracted an offer of help from another motorist, which Brian declined.

The next thing Brian recalls is waking up inside an ambulance as its sirens started to blare. He thought it was his alarm going off and tried to sit up. 'I need to get ready for work', he said. 'You're not going to work today', he heard.

Brian had been discovered about 5 a.m., unconscious on the side of the road, by an off-duty policeman. It was a cold June morning and Brian was warm when found, so the policeman assumed he had not been there for long. Brian told the policeman to call his dad.

As he gathered his thoughts, Brian recalled that white Commodore. Had it run him down after the traffic light altercation?

No. He had been hit by a truck. It pulled up just as the ambulance was turning to depart. The driver explained he may have dozed off while driving, waking when the truck hit a pothole earlier that morning. They had seen the ambulance on their return journey and decided to check...

Brian spent three days in hospital. His helmet was crushed and shattered, and with his bouts of unconsciousness, the hospital's focus was on the impact to his head. His scans showed nothing sinister. He was discharged, feeling extremely sore.

The pain was so severe that the next day he went to the doctor. 'Just bruising that will ease', he was told. Brian asked about physiotherapy, but the doctor did not feel it would help. Brian was convinced it was worth an appointment, so he went to see Geoff, his physio. After a quick inspection, Brian was told, 'I will not touch you until you get more scans'.

By coincidence, a sports physician, Mark, was at the physio clinic that day. As Brian and Mark talked, Brian learned that Mark had been mentored by John, the same close family friend who had helped Brian deal with his asthma.

First, Brian underwent a bone scan, which showed that some of his vertebrae were heavily bruised. He was told not to leave; his CT scan was expedited. It confirmed six crush fractures, with each vertebra losing around 10 per cent height due to the impact.

After a couple of weeks' resting, Brian commenced light exercise in a pool, finding that swimming improved his movement. It became Brian's salvation, under the loving watch of his dad, Gavin, who never missed a 5 a.m. pick-up for his precious son.

Brian was off work for eight months, battling back from his injuries. He was deeply moved by the strength of community support: 'During my sick leave many staff, parents and students displayed acts of kindness to myself and my family that will be forever remembered and cherished.'

Brian put enormous effort into his rehabilitation under Mark's guidance. Mark said, 'The way you feel immediately after swimming is what you can achieve. We will focus your rehab efforts to help you feel like that more consistently.'

It was nearly seven years before Brian was able to resume his beloved running.

I will forever remember and cherish Brian's kindness in coming in to share his and his father's stories. Brian kept reaching out to me through my recovery journey with offers of support and companionship. His courage and humility helped reinforce my foundation.

I am convinced care is amplified when it is welcomed with humility and grace. It is most powerful when it is embraced. During my recovery, so many angels reached out to me – and I learned to let them in. The connections created will remain special, at least to me, for the rest of my days.

Angels are all around you – you just need to find it within yourself to reach out and to accept the help that is offered.

The ability to reach out and in is like your own set of bellows. Practise using them – because nothing can stoke your embers faster than a good set of bellows squeezed well.

The world is rich in kindness when you look for it.

Become a fraction stronger

- Are you comfortable asking for help?
- Can you name the people in your life who have been sources of light and strength in your times of hardship?
- Have you ever experienced someone unexpectedly paying you a kindness? How did that make you feel?
- Who could you reach out to for strength and inspiration right now?
- How could you soften into the help that is available to you and allow it to take hold?
- Has there been a time in your life when you've resisted help that is offered, or suffered in silence? How might things have been different if you had instead embraced others?
- Do you have a trusted support network? If not, how might you develop one?

Chapter 7

Applying effort

'It's not about winning at the Olympic Games; it's about trying to win. The motto is faster, higher, stronger, not fastest, highest, strongest. Sometimes it's the trying that matters and so I think everyone that got out there and pursued their dreams is a little bit of a victor tonight.'

– Bronte Campbell OAM

One of my first constructive thoughts as I waded through the shock news from the medical team on that first day was, 'I am going to give this recovery my absolute best shot'. I encouraged myself with positive ideas: 'Other people have achieved amazing things from much more difficult situations', and 'This is an opportunity to demonstrate character; prove your true colours by taking up the challenge'.

But that was only the first day.

That was before a five-hour operation. Before waking up to exhaustion and incredible aching that transformed into streaks of sharp pain with any movement at all. With feet that felt alien. I think only 'feedback' adequately describes the disturbing nerve-damage-induced sensation of numbness and confusion that came from my legs. Not the constructive kind, more like a microphone-in-front-of-the-amp style of feedback.

On that second day, I felt defeated. I was struggling to give smiling my best shot, never mind pursuing the exceptional outcomes I'd resolved on before my surgery.

Breakfast was delivered and I started to incline the bed to its sitting position, the movement triggering shockwaves of pain across my back. I stopped the bed. The pain was too intense, both from the movement and because it felt like the bed was folding right under my wound site, inflicting pressure – my body didn't have the capability to adapt to the movement of the bed. I scrambled to locate the controller for my patient-controlled analgesia (PCA) and its precious liquid pain relief. The PCA provided a constant infusion of pain medication and, at the press of a button, discharged a predetermined bolus on-demand. I had fervid demand.

I focused on controlling my breathing and settling the adrenalin, on taking a moment to think. I knew I had to get through this step if I wanted to progress.

I counted down the minutes while the PCA pump was locked out, waiting for the light to confirm its relief was available again. I took a dose to shield me through the next movement. I flattened the bed to its original position. I strained to push myself up towards the head of the bed two inches. I couldn't move. My body was drenched with sweat, sticking me to the bed sheets, and I had insufficient mobility or strength to wriggle at all.

My left arm was completely useless. It was swathed in bandaging and temporary splints from the fingers to just beyond my elbow and it seemed to be tangled in a sling. Where had that come from? I couldn't remember any arm sling yesterday. And the cast looked different – I had a vague memory that they had put a cast on my left forearm yesterday, but this temporary cast looked different and was so cumbersome.

My right arm had at least three sets of intravenous (IV) tubes hanging out of it – including the precious PCA pump – constraining and complicating its movements. My lower legs were wrapped in a set of pressurised sleeves that I would later learn was called an intermittent pneumatic compression device, applying firm, massage-style pressure to my legs every 20 seconds or so.

I found a position on the side of the bed for my right hand to grasp so I could use it to push myself up the bed. Nothing. My legs couldn't provide any meaningful help, and I couldn't move. I paused to gather my breath again, and dosed myself with PCA. I experimented with glute squeezes and hip wriggles. *What movements can I manage?* I waited for the PCA machine to unlock, then squeezed its precious button. And I tried again. Straining from head to toe, pushing with all my right arm's might, I tried to wriggle myself a centimetre or so up the bed. I waited for the PCA unlock and repeated the exercise twice more before I was defeated. That was all I was going to manage. Now to try and sit up again.

I waited for the PCA to unlock. I squeezed the button and counted to ten, as I had discovered that seemed to help. Then I started to incline the bed, bracing myself through the pain. As the bed inclined, I felt myself seeping back down the bed. At least half the hard-won gains were relinquished because my legs were unable to hold me in position when confronted with gravity.

Those readers who know hospital beds might recall they offer more a sun lounge recline than a sitting position. It was an uncomfortable position that seemed to be jamming pressure into my wound site and my deeply bruised lower back. It felt like hell.

As I tried to eat breakfast, I realised I could barely swallow food in that position. I didn't have the strength to lift myself off the bed at all, and the angles seemed to mean that the food was catching in my throat. I was starving but suddenly repulsed by eating. It deflated my hopes and distanced my goals.

Around this time, or perhaps it was in the blur of the night before, I was introduced to my new companion: the spirometer. Using it diligently could avoid complications such as post-operative pneumonia, and by extension that meant it helped me get better. As often as I could, and at least every 30 minutes, I needed to practise five to ten deep breaths into it to protect my lung capacity. It sounds simple, but in my weakened condition the deep breaths were tiring. It hurt to sit the bed up to do the exercises, and breathing to capacity caused waves of back pain.

Move, just move

I was desperate to get better. I had to rediscover my resolve to pursue my exceptional outcome. I summonsed the angel of effort. And that angel told me to move, just move.

In those first days, even the smallest of movements was challenging. My left arm was nearly useless, even though I quickly discarded the sling it had been in. My right arm was significantly compromised by the tubes hanging out of it. I had no real capacity to move my legs well in bed, especially when they were wrapped up inside the pneumatic compression device. I had practically no muscle response in my left foot, which was soon placed in a 'resting night splint' – a contraption built by my occupational therapist. This splint placed the foot in a constant 'neutral' position, due to my inability to hold this position. The aim was to protect the foot from further damage; without it, the muscles would have contracted, reducing my recovery prospects.

My biggest issue of all was the vastness of the pain. It was exhausting. I remember a friend coming in to see me on day two or three and simply saying, 'Oh my lord, what have you done you silly thing'. I remember the look in his eyes that conveyed what a mess he saw before him as much as his words.

When I wasn't moving, everything ached despite the heavy pain medication being dripped into me. Any movements sent shockwaves of pain through my body. I needed a minute or two, and additional pain relief, to psych myself up for more intense positional shifts such as rolling onto my side or sitting up on the side of the bed. Any material movements triggered a minute of dizziness due to the benign paroxysmal positional vertigo that I was suffering as a side effect of my head knock. I remember sweating profusely, all the time. I couldn't remember ever sweating this much.

It wasn't until the second week of my recovery that I noticed the pain in my ribs from the three fractured ribs. Until that point, the stabbing nerve pain stemming from my vertebrae fractures and the deep surgery incisions through my back muscles had simply overwhelmed everything else.

'Move, just move' was the mantra I used to push through all these moments. Mentally, all I could think was: 'Don't go backwards. It's hard enough as it is. Your chances are so slim. Do not, do not, have a setback. I don't care how much it hurts, breathe deeply, protect your lungs. Move, protect your muscles. I don't care how much it hurts, take the harder option, just move.' I coaxed myself to endure these tough moments to reach better moments ahead.

Andy, my main physiotherapist in RBWH Acute Care, gave me valuable clarity in those first days: 'For the next year or beyond, recovery is your full-time job. Focus all your energy on it. And you will need ongoing maintenance for the rest of your life. Prepare for it.' Life was going to be hard now and hard later, but early effort had the potential of paying itself back many times over. I regularly thought of Andy's words when my resolve was fading. I committed mentally for the long haul.

That commitment meant I regularly got compliments such as 'You are the hardest working person here' as I proceeded through my various phases of rehabilitation. I was in a hole that I did not like, and I concluded the only way I was going to get back to a happier place was by embracing the help of physiotherapists and my other specialists. I put all available energy into those physio sessions and enjoyed praise for my determination.

Invent and adapt

Andy told me I had to move my feet as much as I could. He gave me movements to practise whenever I could. In hospital I wiggled, rolled and tapped my feet and toes at every opportunity – initially just in bed, then as I progressed, sitting up. At PAH GARU it was a regular part of my gym workouts.

Once I got home from hospital, refining these dorsiflexion (foot) exercises led to my proudest invention, utilising an old pair of Singapore Airlines slippers. The slippers were backless and easy to slip on, which was a key enabler of success. Putting on shoes took significant energy for many months after my accident, and I simply wouldn't have repeated this crucial exercise routine often enough it if required shoes.

I taped a plastic rod to the end of each slipper, perpendicular to the shoe, facing outwards, which enabled me to track my improvement. At least four times a day – sometimes every waking hour – I'd put on those slippers and sit down on a dining chair. I placed a cereal box on the ground in front of me, side-on, which had a target I had marked on its front. The box had to be a certain distance away from me, as I couldn't raise the toes of either foot off the ground if my feet were directly below my knees. (I still can't raise the left if it is in this position.) I would then lift the front of my foot to reach the target on the box using the rod on the end of the slipper as my guide, keeping my heel on the ground. The rod would track up the front of the box, which helped me to monitor and sustain the quality of my exercises. Over time I increased the number of repetitions I could manage, and

I was able to reduce the distance away from me that the box needed to be placed for me to reach the target height.

My outpatient physio checked the improvement at my weekly outpatient catch-ups. She was pleased with the sustained improvement, but then she noticed a developing problem. The nerve damage had impacted the strength and functionality of my feet, and the movement that was returning was concentrated towards the outside muscles. The more I strained to improve, the more my feet – especially the left – were everting. The stronger lateral muscles were responding much more quickly to the exercises, causing the outside of each foot to take over. The exercises need to be changed.

The slippers were reversed so that the rods now faced inwards, not outwards. Targets and repetitions were reset lower so that I could focus specifically on these weaker medial muscles. The cereal box was relocated to be on the inside of my feet as I did my exercises. It was deflating to be barely capable of raising the front of my foot again – I was even worse than when I first started, because I was now isolating the weakest muscles on the inside of my foot. But I knew this intervention by the physio was an important reset to protect my longer-term improvement.

Applying effort is within our control

Effort is a powerful lever in our recovery or development. It helps us remain connected to our sense of purpose. It provides the opportunity to fly our true colours, and it leads to respect. Respect from others and, most importantly, ourselves.

Positive feedback reinvigorates effort.

Effort powers the transition from our current state towards our goals. Trying changes our mindset – it provides new perspectives.

Positive effort helps us break negative momentum and move back towards belief, and that is an essential ingredient of perseverance.

I knew that to sustain my effort towards my identified goal of recovery, I needed to set myself smaller goals and identify the tasks that made up those goals. I had to develop the momentum that would nourish belief and effort. Forming habits to focus energy on the tasks that supported my goals was an approach that I could control and sustain. Small actions enable you to:

· make a start
· focus your limited energy on your highest priorities
· be forgiving – allow missteps! Gain comfort from the fact that it is OK to be wrong. Not much is lost and so much is gained – you have started, you have tried, you have new information
· be flexible – you can keep reassessing your goals and task priorities as you improve
· be gracious – celebrate and reward everything. Intent and effort matter most.

And by trying, you will have liberated more possibility!

Small actions are readily adjusted for trial and error. You can invent and adjust as you make progress, as I did for these critical exercises supporting the recovery of my feet. In time, you can refine the precision of your goals, as I did. But to get moving, aspirational goals are appropriate. As Simon Sinek says, 'It doesn't matter when we start. It doesn't matter where we start. All that matters is that we start.' Just start!

There will be uncertainties and setbacks over time. Utilise your angels – including positive feedback – to restock your energy. Foster the vision of the possible you have been working on, and fight for it. Take steps towards it – any steps will do. They do not need to be perfect. Move, just move.

Trying matters most...

I love sport. I always enjoyed participating, thinking about how to improve my own game and the team around me. I am incredibly proud to have played in so many fabulous teams over the years; their collective spirit is part of my life fabric. I strived for success and revelled in the victories, but I was primarily motivated by questions such as: How do we generate and sustain effort? How do we improve?

I was driven by that intense satisfaction of having stretched towards an aspirational outcome, both in terms of preparation and performance. Some days you are just outshone by a superior performance; some days you didn't quite play your best, and the reasons are difficult to identify. What mattered most to me was the sense of willing myself, trying to reach high standards.

Of all the world sporting events, the Summer Olympics captivates me the most. Diverse individuals competing across a wide array of sporting disciplines, consistently delivering stories of incredible valour, all celebrated within the sense of a global community. I find it uniquely compelling to watch.

As someone who was an average athlete, I deeply respect the application it takes to become an elite athlete. The commitment to training. Accepting that by aiming high, you may fall short of your goals. To potentially 'fail' based on the critics' expectations or measures.

Winners are celebrated, but so are those who simply step into the arena and give their all. We get the benefit of watching, and being inspired by, people pursuing their dreams.

Bronte and Cate Campbell OAM are champion Australian swimmers in the freestyle sprint events. Heading into the 2016 Summer Olympics in Rio de Janeiro, Bronte was the reigning world champion in the 50 m and 100 m freestyle. On the first day of the Olympics meet, the sisters swam blistering times as the Australian team set a new world record in winning the 4 × 100 m relay. The sisters were strong favourites to secure individual medals in the 100 m freestyle event, especially after Cate lowered the individual Olympic record time in her heat and then in the semi-final.

In the final, Cate swam ahead of her own record for perhaps 75 m before fading and getting swamped late. Bronte missed bronze by fractions of a second. After the race, Bronte provided us with the inspiring quote I have shared to open this chapter. It represents all the things I admire about the Olympics, and how I feel about applying effort towards any endeavour.

In 2021, these two champions put themselves into the arena again, winning gold and lowering the world record in the women's 4 × 100 m freestyle relay. Cate also won gold in the women's 4 × 100 m medley relay and Bronte won bronze in the mixed 4 × 100 m medley relay. It was cheering Cate to individual bronze in the women's 100 m freestyle that made me especially jubilant – testimony of her willingness to try and her ability to cope with disappointment.

If you are seeking personal growth, or coming back from trauma like I was, I am convinced it is the effort that matters. Your character is forged by the resolve to try, and perhaps fail, in the pursuit of becoming 'faster, higher, stronger' or the relevant equivalent. I love the way Deborah Moggach puts this: 'The only real failure is the failure to try, and the measure of success is how we cope with disappointment.'

I desperately wanted to recover fully, but it was improving my strength, my balance, my functionality one small fraction after another that would accumulate to make a difference. It was the rigour of applying the attitude and effort to make improvement possible that counted. Falling short didn't matter. Trying did.

That was what I could control.

Be like Chi

I met Chi about six months into my rehabilitation journey. For about 18 months we would see each other as my physiotherapy finished and hers started. If I ever sensed my effort waning, I just needed to look to Chi and her commitment. Perhaps she might say we had a positive impact on each other – I'd be proud of that. Because Chi applied herself as diligently as any peer I saw during my recovery journey.

As a five-year-old, Chi had sailed from Vietnam with her family on a bashed-up fishing boat. It took two months before they reached their new home – Australia. Life was hard but effort was rewarded, and they slowly built themselves up from where they started, which was from nothing. It was an opportunity that her family grabbed with both hands, that they treasured. The challenges developed Chi's strength of character and her resilience.

Chi worked hard to generate a comfortable and independent life with her two beautiful teenage children. She was loving her career change into real estate – the last two years of work had been some of her most rewarding. Then life changed.

At 2 p.m. on 1 March 2019, Chi was at a local shopping centre dealing with some real estate appointments. As Chi walked, she developed the weirdest numb, tingling sensation on her upper left arm. It felt like a muscle ache from strenuous activity, but without the exercise! She had no idea what it was, so Chi massaged it a bit and kept moving through her meetings.

But the feeling got worse and worse, until it was sufficiently bad for her to think, 'This isn't right, I should get home'. She drove the ten minutes back to her home.

At home, Chi sat down and applied some Deep Heat to the area, hoping this would ease her mystery muscle ache. Then, as she stood up, her movement was unsteady. She felt paralysed and couldn't walk. She thought, 'Oh no, I better call an ambulance' as she sat back down.

Chi's children and partner laughed at her. Chi never got sick, and suddenly she was acting like she had been shot or something. It was surreal.

'No, it is serious – I can't move.' Chi was scared shitless.

Chi called the ambulance. She was in PAH by 4 p.m. She felt physically helpless as she lay paralysed in the emergency department. 'How has this happened to me in just two hours?' she thought. She could not move; she could not feed herself. She felt that she could not do anything. She was sent for a wide range of scans as they tried to establish what had happened. They found some inflammation in her spinal cord. The neurosurgeon showed her that a large area of her spinal cord was white, then explained that it should be clear.

Chi had suffered a spinal cord stroke. They are extremely rare, constituting about 1 per cent of all strokes. She was put on an intra-venous anti-inflammatory drug to alleviate the spinal blockage. She required three weeks of bed rest while the inflammation reduced. She could not have moved if she wanted to. It was a difficult period of waiting, wondering how this random event had hit her. Something that the specialists could not adequately explain.

Chi desperately did not want to permanently lose her mobility, and she wanted to minimise the risk of this freak, unexplainable event happening again. Chi used this fear as motivation.

Once Chi could commence her rehabilitation effort, the physios would put her in a wheelchair and push her to the gym. She commenced walking with the support of a wheelie-walker and two physiotherapists. Then she moved onto the parallel bars. She worked hard to succeed, to grasp the opportunities. As she had all her life.

Chi pursued her rehabilitation with all her willpower, and after three months was able to relocate home. But she had to use the wheelchair, especially if she left the house, and she didn't enjoy the way being in the wheelchair made her feel or the way she was treated.

It took Chi about four months of sustained effort to graduate from her wheelchair to two Canadian crutches. She now felt more capable of leaving the house, but still required help from family or friends to support her. Her balance and strength remained compromised, so she needed someone to walk alongside for safety.

Chi was unlucky to be inflicted with an extremely rare condition. It scared the hell out of her, and it changed her physical capabilities. Everything takes longer than before. She cannot dash out to the shops to grab something for her greatest passion and talent – cooking. She can't weed the garden because of her balance issues. Chi cannot keep up when walking with her children and feels dispirited falling behind.

She works as hard as anyone that I've met on my journey, leaving no stone unturned to recover. She lives with the fear that she could have another stroke and makes sure she uses that as motivation to live her best life, to make the most of each moment, to be grateful for what she has and to reach her most exceptional outcome. She told me:

'On the one hand, you could feel sorry for yourself and say:

"Why me, why did this happen to me? Of all the people in the world I lived healthy, I exercised, I ate well, I didn't drink or smoke. Why me? Woe is me."

Or you can look at it and go:

"Wow, how lucky am I? I am walking – maybe a little bit of pain; yes, I'm a bit wobbly… but I can cook for myself."

Our challenges open our eyes up to another world.'

Overcoming adversity, such a physical injury, requires significant, targeted effort. I assure you that effort is worth it. It gives you self-worth. It provides some level of control over your destiny. And it generates valuable bonds with those who treat you – and with your family, your friends: the angels who enable you to do exceptional things.

Applying effort is totally in your control, and even the smallest acts can change your circumstances and perspective. It is a powerful lever in your recovery or development.

Celebrate your effort and your outcomes as you stretch for your possible outcome. Focus on the feelings of self-respect your effort generates. Forgive missteps – the experiences they yield outweigh the downsides.

Be your own angel.

Become a fraction stronger

- Thinking back to a difficult situation you have faced, can you recall the effort you applied to overcome the problem?
- How did you feel before and after applying that effort? Did you feel the burden of emotions lighten once you had taken positive action?
- What is a longer-term goal you could focus all your effort on achieving?
- What small action could you take today to bring you closer to what you want?
- What if you repeated and sustained that small action, then supplemented that effort with other small actions? How would that accelerate your progress?

Chapter 8
Fostering belief

'Wherever you go, go with all your heart.'
– Confucius

I am a disciple of imagination. Of dreams. I am convinced that if we empower an open mind, it can help us visualise and aim for almost anything. I like to think of liberating possibility as the 'head' – or ideas – component of reaching our exceptional outcomes. Fostering belief is the 'heart'. The conviction.

Possibility provides you with a platter of outcomes: a platter that you can extend and refresh by embracing uncertainty and exploring pathways, by applying effort. Goals – aspirational or targeted – are chosen from that platter. Belief is the genesis of reaching for those goals and provides the sustenance that allows you to adapt and persevere.

In my experience I've found that if you want to make a change in your circumstances, you need to form a powerful vision of where you want to be. Believe in the potential of that outcome. Plan, but do not be fixated on the path – because once you start the journey, new pathways will unfold.

From the moment I received my shock news, I fought to develop, cling to and then refine images of how I might cope and succeed. I summonsed all the mettle I could from my life and work experiences. I plucked belief from my recollections of other relevant successes. People who had achieved incredible outcomes from tough circumstances: Lucy, friends.

I visualised the young Alan Marshall living a life punctuated with triumphs and joy, despite dealing with significant physical deficits in an era when there was much less support. Riding that horse, Starlight, exuding unbounded joy. I wanted my spirit to remain free, as Alan's had.

I visualised a version of Karni Liddell, whose story I could only vaguely recall. I pictured Karni as a smiling young child being strapped into some home-made walking contraption, and I reconstructed my own version of a story of how that child grew to accomplish amazing things against great odds. I didn't focus on her worthy outcomes of being a Paralympian, champion of compassion or inspirer of change. My heart sought and found connection with a story of persistence. Someone who didn't select their goals only once they had dismissed those that were too lofty. An image of character; a person who refused to yield when the road ahead was almost intolerably tough. A journey of great achievement ignited by not much more than the innocence of a child and the unwavering faith of loving parents.

I didn't see myself as a potential Paralympian. I wasn't aiming to inspire anyone (beyond being an appropriate role model for my kids – Luke, Imogen and Charlie). I just wanted to put my heart and soul *into the journey* with the same passion as the person who had achieved those outcomes.

This accumulated array of thoughts and memories provided me with the belief that I could flourish – or at least give myself every chance. I could strive for my preferred recovery among the platter of potential outcomes, and attitude would be the main dish on my plate.

Belief was my keel, providing stability whenever I wobbled. And in the first few weeks I wobbled a lot. Maybe I could poetically portray that week as the feature roller-coaster in an emotional theme park if I had taken better notes. I won't try and fill in details I can't adequately recall, but every day I navigated a range of rough conditions, and I often struggled.

On the calming side there was the kindness of my visitors, amazing care from so many of the staff, and the text messages of encouragement. Then there was the unsteadiness ensuing from the pain and exhaustion caused by any movement, disrupted sleep, the isolation of being abandoned regularly in various parts of the hospital (let's just say there are opportunities for greater efficiency), and complications with my catheter that I'll spare you from reading.

These tribulations absorbed energy and tested my will. They threatened to wash away belief. They were the daily chop I had to sail through, on top of the giant wave and current that also smashed into me, that fully tested the resolve of my tack.

'We're going to get you up'

My first Monday night in acute care was one of my worst hospital 'sleeps'. Whether it was the fear and uncertainty I was battling with, or just the hallucinatory side effects of pain medication, I had the most vivid and scary dreamlike experience. I thought I was awake half the night, hearing shouts of pain and torment from a nearby patient together with the medical responses that go with that. It rattled me.

Consequently, I was very much 'on edge' Tuesday morning when physio Andy arrived. I am sure we exchanged some polite greetings before he ripped the band-aid off: 'We're going to stand you up'. As I mentioned in chapter 2, my wish was to defer: 'But I am too weak and exhausted'. I don't recall if that was verbalised or I expressly fought the decision, but I remember feeling there was no chance of me doing this and I didn't want to do it. In case you haven't noticed, it takes a lot to get me to that point! The thing is, Andy wasn't providing the option of 'tomorrow', and I wanted to get better 'today'. I firmly believed that I had to find the fortitude to get through moments like this to get better. Andy fortified me.

But despite Andy's support, I didn't feel capable. It didn't make the fear subside because I had no faith that I could manage the task. Andy explained he would get another physio to ensure I was safe. I can't honestly say that he convinced me, but between his conviction that it was possible and my appreciation that it was an essential milestone, we got it done.

Sometimes we just need to find a way to adopt someone's belief, and Andy believed in me.

But before I could stand, Andy had to teach me how to sit.

This took a little bit of trial and error that morning and induced a lot of dizziness and spasms of pain. The routine that we discovered worked for me was this:

1. I was rolled onto my right side. (My left side had to be facing up because of its injuries.)
2. Through a series of wriggles, I'd get myself close to the edge of the bed.
3. The bed was inclined to its maximum angle. Even with the headstart of this elevation, I barely had the strength to push to sitting.
4. My legs would be shuffled to the cusp of the bed.
5. I'd push myself up to sitting using rotation. As my legs swung downwards, they would lever my body from lying on the bed to sitting on the side of the bed. It triggered sharp pain.

Before any of that started, there was the process of a nurse or physio freeing my legs from their constraints. I would then sort out the IV tubes on my right arm so that I could roll onto that side without getting in a tangle. I would locate and place the various controls (bed and pain relief) in a position where I could access them during the movements. After each movement, I needed rest to recover from the dizziness and fatigue. I'd also top up on pain relief to get me through each excruciating step.

In the first day or so I needed a physio or nurse on hand to make sure I didn't over-rotate because of the lack of strength and control in my torso. Once I was safe to sit up by myself, it was liberating, especially for the purposes of eating. It was something I could do. It built belief as well as strength.

On that first Tuesday, once the minute or so of dizziness passed, Andy and his colleague talked me through standing. They were going to lift me and support me as my feet hit the ground and I would reach forward to the handles of the rollator that would support me. I was petrified. But it worked as they said, and I was up.

It felt like an out of body experience because I was unsteady and misfiring – the mixed electrical signals caused by the nerve damage meant my body was in chaos. My feet felt so distant, my legs were shaking wildly and my arms were twitching. I was neurologically confused.

Then Andy said, 'Let's take a walk'. At least my ears worked!

I was petrified about standing, let alone walking. This wasn't listed in the brochure.

With a physio on each side, I walked about three metres, reaching just outside the doorway of my room. I had no idea what my feet were doing, and it was consuming a lot of energy to get my legs to stagger forwards. A lot of my body weight was supported by the rollator, via my forearms. My hands felt welded by distress onto the rollator handles.

Mirroring my malfunctioning electrical signals, my emotions were totally mixed up. It was uplifting that I could move but devastating how confused and difficult that movement was. I felt disconnected in so many ways.

With each progressive day we'd walk a few more metres. A fraction stronger. Each day.

Start by getting through today

If standing up was a giant wave rocking my belief, lying down was the rip that seemed to be constantly dragging belief away. I associated lying down with putting my lungs at risk. It reinforced the immobility of my feet and the numbness of my legs.

Mentally I made the regular ASIA testing of my legs and feet the focus of my first mini milestone. I knew it was ill-conceived, but I wanted my damage to miraculously pass as my bruising eased, as the muscle shock reduced. I tried to constantly move my feet and flex the toes, the ankle, with almost a manic regularity. And with each ASIA test I hoped to hear improved numbers.

But there was no improvement. Just minor variations in testing consistency from nurse to occupational therapist to physio to spinal specialist. Minor variations in whether I might manage a flicker of movement.

If anything, from Tuesday to Friday my assessed foot movement faded. The ASIA tests of Thursday and Friday yielded a series of confidence blows as I consistently heard scores of zero for my left big toe and one for left foot and right big toe movement. The cold numbness in my legs was haunting, and by Friday I was on the edge of panic.

That Friday was the toughest day. I was onto about the third iteration of my dripped pain relief as the doctors sought to get on top of my constant pain. The dosage was making me feel totally out of it and on the edge of being chemically (mentally) imbalanced. My feet and legs were so heavy and numb, and getting colder by the minute. My catheter had been removed at about 4 a.m., but, worryingly, I had no sensation of my bladder filling or the urge to wee. Fears such as 'Will I need a catheter for life?' were swilling about.

Perhaps I could have calmed myself by recalling the Harper Lee quote, 'Things are never as bad as they seem'. Maybe I tried – because it is the style of thought I often channelled in my corporate career when my challenges seemed overwhelming. It was all I could manage to focus on taking each moment as it came, while not giving up on all future hope.

At some point, physio Andy came in and said he needed to perform a full ASIA test. He started with the normal large muscle tests, my feet and toes getting their normal zeros and ones. Then he described how he needed to perform sensory tests on me. First it was just lightly touching me in different places with some cotton wool to see if I could sense the touch. Then Andy performed a blunt/sharp test on me, where he poked me with a specific testing pin: square plastic on one end, pointed metal on the other. He prodded me up and down the line of various nerves to estimate my spinal cord damage. I had to respond if the poke provoked a sharp or blunt sensation. Typically, the patient is blindfolded, as I was for a follow-up ASIA sensory test in late April. But when Andy performed the test that Friday, all he had to do was lay the bed flat. I was so immobile I had no ability to see what Andy was doing. No blindfold was required.

Even on my quads and hamstrings I was uncertain whether the sensation was sharp or blunt – another blow to my hopes. For the previous two days I had felt optimism that these muscles weren't impacted, given I had learned that they were getting five out of five on the ASIA movement test. As Andy progressed towards my feet, I was feeling increasingly deflated and confused. I was guessing for almost every prod whether a sharp or blunt sensation was stimulated, especially around my ankles and over the tops of my feet.

The test shell-shocked me. Afterwards, I was catastrophising about what the sensory confusion meant when my attention was diverted from my own woes. I learned of the mass shooting of innocent people who were sharing their daily prayers in Christchurch. It rocked me emotionally that somebody could plan and do such an evil thing. It reminded me of the fragility of life and that I was blessed with an opportunity if I could just persevere.

In all this turmoil, I was left clinging to my last semblance of positive intent. Even though I had made important progressions such as sitting and standing during that first week, it felt like my journey had gotten tougher. Each successive day delivered evidence that my spinal cord damage was worse than I had hoped. The experience of the full ASIA test and my catheter failure on that Friday were deep blows. They eroded my belief and distanced me from my goals. My world seemed to be falling apart.

The temporary distraction of the Christchurch tragedy provided the pause I needed to rally my grit. I reassured myself that it was just a disappointing test, on a difficult day. It hadn't eroded the utility of striving for my mini-goals, such as wiggling my toes and flexing my feet. I focused on these small, regular efforts, endeavouring to stimulate movement and keep alive the chance of future improvement. To hang in there. To not give up.

I reached again for my most powerful internal tool of those deteriorating days: the refusal to concede. This made me think again of the strength of my beautiful neighbour, Clare, as I had done on my first day when I was grasping for irrepressible inspiration.

Tomorrow is a new day

Clare's story has many twists and turns – even just the abridged version could easily fill a whole chapter. I have focused on the key events that inspired me. Perhaps one day Clare and Craig will release their own complete version for you to enjoy. The story is too beautiful to leave unprinted.

Over the course of about two years, Clare showed me just how strong a person's fighting spirit can be, and how you can face any challenge with grace and humility. In May 2015 it was revealed she had Stage 4 Hodgkin's lymphoma impacting her neck, lungs, back and bone marrow. The news devastated her, but she stepped up to the challenge – six months of chemotherapy. After that, life returned to normal. For a while.

An abnormal blood result in August 2016 uncovered acute myeloid leukemia. Clare had another, more difficult battle ahead.

She fought her way through numerous rounds of chemotherapy and full-body radiation therapy. She persevered through the uncertainty of securing suitable donor bone marrow. She endured months of isolation from her family, confined to hospital in her neutropenic (no immunity) state. She did it all in her own selfless, no-fuss manner.

The part of Clare's story that hit me hardest transpired around Boxing Day, 2016. I received a text from Clare's husband Craig saying that Clare was feverish and unwell, that her body appeared to be rejecting the donor marrow that she had been desperately waiting for. I vividly recall thinking, 'But Clare has been through so much, she has fought so hard, she has been preparing her body for so long. This can't happen.'

I was worried that it might be one cruelty too many.

Not for Clare. Yet again she refused to concede. Her challenge was so much more complex than mine, but she didn't yield: 'Tomorrow's a new day. I'll probably feel a little bit better.'

Clare mustered that incredible resolve one more time. She found the rhythms and tactics that helped her get through each of those many tough moments to get to better moments ahead. To fight her way back to her treasured family.

And, with time and effort, she fought back to full health.

Clare's prevailing spirit put her firmly in my spotlight when I was desperately seeking to bolster my belief. My challenges were real; they weren't going away just because they were less difficult than Clare's. But if Clare could keep finding belief through all the obstacles of her journey, I must be able to as well.

When my belief was fading, reflecting on Clare's resolve reminded me that if we do not concede in the tough moments, we give time for our hopes to happen. Clare's story comforted me that any setbacks that hit me would not be decisive – they were not the end. They could not extinguish my hope, even if they amplified the extent of the challenge. I needed to keep willing myself to take up that challenge. I needed to think like Sonny Kapoor: 'Everything will be alright in the end, and if it is not alright, it is not the end.'

I had to work extremely hard to sustain a sense of possibility – that 'I could do it'. Perhaps the most powerful internal tool I had in those deteriorating early days was the refusal to concede, emboldened by the inspiration of Clare.

Angels bring belief

As important and powerful as my own positive reflections were, I am deeply grateful these were extended by the actions of others. Over my first weekend in hospital, I had three crucial visits over three days that instilled new belief.

As you know, over that first week I was losing movement and sensation in my feet. And I was losing hope. On that bleak, stormy Friday evening, Greg, my cousin-in-law, made a surprise visit before flying home to Perth.

He arrived shortly after they had re-inserted the catheter because my bladder wouldn't work, so I was feeling very low.

A physiotherapist who runs a successful business in workplace injury management, Greg had a good understanding of trauma injuries like mine. He wanted to check on me and provide support. He tracked down my wife's details through the family network and found out where I was. Despite the deadline of a looming flight, a massive thunderstorm that created traffic havoc, and having to locate me in an unfamiliar hospital, he came to see me. His endorsement of my treatment, the guidance I was receiving and, most importantly, what I visualised achieving strengthened my belief.

Over the weekend, I was visited by two people with personal or family experience of similar injuries to mine, with stories I have already shared.

First, Brian, who I introduced in chapter 6, gave me the book *Legacy* with his powerful inscription and described his successful journey back from multiple back fractures.

The next day, the coach of my eldest boy's cricket team, Steely, dropped in with a card and gift that he and the team had sorted. I was one of their regular cricket scorers, as I had been for their fighting win over Ashgrove the afternoon before my accident. Steely told me the story of his niece Ellen fracturing her back on a bus while backpacking in Egypt. (You'll remember that from chapter 2.)

Importantly, I didn't seek to find gaps in the stories of Brian and Ellen – of how they might be different or easier than mine. I focused on the similarities, and that allowed the stories to provide maximum belief. In negotiator talk, we describe this as making the gap appear smaller.

Greg, Brian and Steely reinforced and extended the belief that I was so desperately trying to build. They encouraged me to believe that I, too, could achieve my own exceptional recovery. They enabled me to build a substantial bridge of belief that connected me to those visions of my best possible outcome I was clinging to.

Accept that there might be a pathway

Belief connects where we are to where we aspire to reach. It's the internal framing that links our imagination to our foundations.

Belief illuminates the possible pathways available to us. I accepted the ambiguity in that path. I didn't seek to identify every step. I reasoned that those big gaps in the 'how' could be valuable at times. The path can and must change. Tackling those areas of uncertainty between each step would bring powerful opportunities, liberating new possibility. Belief was the nucleus of my recovery, from which I could generate the vision and attitude that guided me through my uncertainty. It was the strong heart that kept my effort circulating.

Belief can come from inside us, and it can be refreshed and extended by those around us. It connects to our purpose, our values. It gives us energy – it sustains that flicker of hope. It convinces us to keep trying, to tackle uncertainty, to overcome demons.

I sustained my belief by routinely:

- reviewing where I was versus my goals, and how I felt
- reflecting on what was working, what needed to change to ensure my efforts were focused on my goals, and to manage how I felt
- refining goals to ensure belief could be sustained. This included delaying goals, cultivating new, smaller goals, and culling goals that no longer fitted.

I went through many phases of setting different mini-goals. For example, during 2019 I decided that I would walk during the pre-game time of my children's sporting events. The night before each game, I'd research where I could walk; then, while they were warming up, I would be walking the local pathways and streets, or just laps of a neighbouring oval. I pushed myself as hard and fast as I could safely manage, ignoring the pain of my slapping feet and jarring back. It wasn't much fun when plovers or magpies swooped me, as I had no ability to move quickly out of the danger zone.

I tracked all my activity in the Strava app so I could see my pace per kilometre, and therefore my progression. Seeing improvement in my results fostered belief that the effort was paving my way towards better outcomes. Positive feedback reinvigorates belief.

Belief is the heartbeat of your journey. It is your guiding angel. Protect and encourage your belief like a good friend, as you use every means possible to reinforce and extend it.

I fought to develop belief and hold onto it with all my strength. I focused my thoughts on others who had overcome hurdles and accomplished great things against the odds. I recalled moments in my own life when I'd surprised myself by what I'd achieved. I used these thoughts and memories to stoke the embers of my belief. To sustain me.

Allow belief to illuminate the possible pathways available to you. Set goals that connect to your possible. Consider your attitude. Belief can be the difference between breaking down and breaking through. Use every means possible to reinforce and extend it.

Become a fraction stronger

- Thinking of your biggest goals, can you identify any thoughts or beliefs that are eroding your confidence in achieving them?
- What are some interim goals you could set to build your belief?
- What have you achieved so far as you work towards your goals?
- Who do you know who has reached a similar goal or overcome a comparable hurdle? What can you learn from them to stoke your own belief?

Chapter 9
Uniting through love

'I've seen and met angels wearing the disguises of ordinary
people living ordinary lives.'
– Tracy Chapman

I had lonely moments in my journey, but I was never truly alone
thanks to the love from my wonderful family. I benefited greatly from
the generosity of our network. My body and spirit were salvaged by
the kind proficiency of Australia's world-class trauma care staff and so
many other medical professionals.

My outcomes were made possible by the countless angels who
guided me through adversity. The encouragement of friends whose
actions spurred and rekindled resolve. The guidance of Lucy and
many others who helped me make good decisions. The interventions
of many ordinary people providing extraordinary care.

Perched at the top of the tree of cherished kindness, one gentle
intervention stands out as my most precious. It was crucial care
I received from my nurse, Nicole, on day nine – when I had lost my
perspective and will.

Love is unifying

Let me quickly recap the timeline to adequately set the scene. I'd crashed on Sunday and battled through the shocks of those first few days. From Wednesday to Friday, my hope had been seeping away with the deteriorating movement in my feet, before the important visits of Greg, Brian and Steely. Collectively they hauled me back from Friday afternoon's dejection by conveying calmness, sharing stories and instilling priceless belief over three consecutive days.

It was now Monday. I was very weak. Movement remained painful and difficult, and my progressions were, at best, modestly heartening. I was sitting up for longer periods each day. I had started to feel slightly more human as I could now (with a nurse helping) get to the bathroom to shower sitting in a chair, even if I could not dry or dress myself. I was managing one short rollator walk in the corridor most days. Perhaps the progress helped me to start that second week with a fraction more hope. But it was only a fraction, and it was about to dissipate.

At the recommendation of a friend, I emailed Bicycle Queensland that morning and asked about any assistance my membership might provide. I found it a really difficult thing to do. This was the first time that I was admitting to anyone how perilous my predicament was. I was reaching out because the last week had taught me that I needed every bit of help I could locate. I was acknowledging to myself that my challenges were far greater than I'd hoped.

I received a swift response directly from the CEO, Anne. Her tone was so genuine and human that it reduced me to tears. For weeks afterwards, if I thought about her email or tried to tell someone about it, I would choke up with emotion.

So, I was feeling emotionally exposed and very fragile about my prospects that Monday morning, when I received a visit that rocked me to my core.

To that point, I'd understood I would not be transferred to the PAH Spinal Injuries Unit, which is the facility treating Queensland's most severe spinal cord injuries. But my condition, as evidenced during that first week, warranted the PAH Spinal Injuries Unit team travelling to RBWH so they could review me. This involved the ASIA strength and sensory testing, plus a range of questions, including about my bladder and bowel functions. They monitored me as I battled to roll in bed, sit up, stand, then 'walk' about ten metres using the rollator as support (with physios guiding me).

At the end of the examination, the head of the unit looked at me gravely. 'We need to put you on our waitlist', he said. 'It's currently three months long.' I was devastated. My best possible recovery was not built around this unfolding event. I knew my damage was serious, but I'd visualised that slim chance of total recovery. In one sentence, that hope felt totally shattered.

After they left, I was a mess, awash with anxiety and fighting back tears. My thoughts were racing through my mind so quickly I had lost all ability to think straight. I was demanding answers of myself I had no ability to give: 'Why am I on the waitlist? How can I adequately progress right now if the waitlist is three months?'

Their assessment was totally incongruent with my hopes and expectations, meaning that I was not capable of processing it as anything apart from terrible news. I was catastrophising what it signalled about my longer-term prospects. Since the crash I had relentlessly been finding and accumulating any rays of hope I could as lanterns guiding me towards possibility, lighting a pathway that might just lead to an exceptional recovery.

Suddenly I felt I was clinging to a lie I had built from my imagination. My world had caved in, and I could not see how I was going to raise those rays of hope again.

I was lonely beyond belief.

My wonderful nurse came into my room to perform her regular checks. Nicole looked at me and seemed to sense all was not well. I felt her gaze become more intent as she asked, 'Are you OK?' That was all it took for my floodgates to open, to unlock a deluge of woe and self-pity.

For 20 minutes or more Nicole listened, consoled, and reset my perspectives. She encouraged me to get moving again; she restocked belief. I'll never forget the time she invested in my mental wellbeing. I will always recall her gentle intervention with genuine warmth and the deepest gratitude. My spirits were boosted by Nicole's exceptional attention over several shifts. No matter how busy she was, she always conveyed an aura of genuine kindness. Nicole exemplifies how the care that emanates from a compassionate heart is one of the most imperishable forces.

I feel deep gratitude towards the countless nurses who tended me over my journey. Perhaps many of them may have been capable of similar empathy, but I do feel that Nicole was the perfect fit for me that day. It was the willingness to gently intervene, to look a fraction deeper and push me – 'Are you OK?' – that limited the extent of my descent in that moment of spiralling despair. Her act of kindness reunited me with hope.

There were many other charitable moments. Visits, messages of support, cutting myself some slack when needed – often with the help of angels like Nicole. I benefited from the generosity of human spirit epitomised by Princess Diana when she said, 'Carry out a random act of kindness, with no expectation of reward, safe in the knowledge that one day someone might do the same for you'.

These angels made choices that helped my journey enormously. A series of important, gentle interventions.

Love arrives unexpectedly

On the second day after the accident, I was dozing, exhausted after standing for the first time with Andy's assistance. I was deflated and confused by how disconnected my legs had felt during that episode, so I was fragile and barely coping when a lady I did not recognise knocked, then entered my room as I stirred. She was bearing flowers and gifts. She introduced herself as Dee, wife of my eldest son's Year 5 teacher Brendan. Dee showed genuine care as she conveyed her and Brendan's shock at the extent of my injuries and their best wishes for my recovery.

Dee let me know that she was a plastic surgeon at the hospital, and she personally wanted to stitch my fingers. I started to gently weep and could barely get any words out as she introduced herself. Her kindness cut right to my heart, exposing all my fragility and sense of woe. Dee carefully cleaned and stitched my fingers as we chatted.

Later that day I told Lucy the story, and I learned that Brendan had been riding in the same area as me that same morning I crashed. Brendan recognised some of the other dads from school standing concernedly at our crash site. As this was not a common route for either group, it was an amazing coincidence of timing. He stopped, checked on who was down and became aware that this looked serious.

Once home, Brendan commenced his own gentle interventions. He rang the leadership of our boys' school and conveyed that I was in a serious way. He prompted the school to monitor the welfare of our two boys over the coming week. Brendan told Dee the story and she decided that she was going to check on me, then see if she could be assigned to stitch me.

I would soon develop much greater appreciation of the quality of Dee's work and the importance of her skill in tending my wounds.

It was a few weeks later that my fingers were released from their bandaged cocoon. I discovered that the little finger of my left hand was constantly curling into a bent ('fist') position. I could not move it back into a straightened position without using my right hand to force its movement. Within seconds of me forcing it straight it would slump back into its curl. It was assessed by a PAH orthopaedic doctor in early April, who expressed concern that tendon damage had been overlooked in the initial scans. Or perhaps the stitching performed at RBWH had caused scarring, impacting the function of the knuckle, or in the worst case, that some tendon damage had been caused by the stitching process. They decided in the first instance they would send me to the hand therapist to see if it might improve, before investigating these worst-case scenarios.

With the help of a moulded plastic hand splint and a series of exercises I had to do every hour or so, the finger recovered its movement. When I went back to the hand therapist two weeks later, she said, 'I was certain that the finger would recover, as the stitching work you had done was by one of the very best doctors'. 'You have heard of the surgeon?' I asked, concluding she had must have read in my file that Dee had done the plastics work. 'Yes, she used to work here, and she does brilliant work', my hand therapist replied.

My finger and its ringside buddy still have a few minor functionality issues, but considering the level of risk I had faced of losing significant mobility or facing additional operations – risks that Dee managed for me – I feel extremely grateful. It is yet another demonstration of how small this world is, how powerful kindness can be, and how gentle interventions can transform trajectory.

As soon as I was discharged, I wrote a note of thanks to Dee and Brendan. I felt very emotional as I typed that note, and reflecting on their care still impacts me today. Love and kindness can come from so many unexpected places. They are just so powerful.

Love can trespass

'Intervention' is a word that can invoke an element of misgiving. Perhaps it is because we tend to use it to describe actions that may be perceived as forceful and invasive, often unwelcome. A trespass into something too personal, or that one opinion too many.

I think I have often associated intervention with relinquishing control, and while I might try and convince myself that I 'don't need to be in control', I suspect I seldom felt fully comfortable in situations in which I had no control at all. On the day of the accident, I didn't feel comfortable about the operation and recovery ahead, but I was able to endure that period of 'no control', knowing that I would wrest back some control via my attitude in the days ahead. To liberate myself for the day, I had to envisage how I might regain an element of control in the future.

Stepping into uncertainty can be daunting in any circumstances, but if we feel we have less control, or no recourse, it takes the uncertainty to a heightened exposure level. Paradoxically, when we do step into that uncertainty, or even fear, it tends to be empowering rather than disempowering. We release ourselves from the weight of a burden. But it is difficult to sustain that sense of surrender, and we naturally drift back inside our fortifications with time.

The blocking or constraining nature of our self-made walls is captured expertly by Rūmī: 'Your task is not to seek for love, but merely to seek and find all the barriers within yourself that you have built against it.' This instinct to barricade makes it harder to receive, and harder to offer, the important interventions that might just turn our moment, our day. If we avoid the desire to resist, if we allow kindness to trespass, then even the most subtle benevolence can provide perpetuating momentum. Visits, words or thoughts that offer just the right touch of distraction, that help us reconnect to our identity and then rebalance our perspective, are so crucial. Embrace them with the love they merit.

Karni Liddell's parents delivered a gentle intervention as they instigated the trajectory that eventually led to two Paralympic medals. It was measured, sustained, and supported with love. It must have taken enormous courage, perhaps driven by a feeling of necessity.

Maybe in my case it was easier. The crushed vertebrae created a clear structural necessity. But I still needed resolve to keep pushing into uncertainty, to trust the many interventions I had in my journey. Recovery-shaping interventions such as my sessions with physio Leanne, relived in chapter 5. The most fundamental intervention on that first day – trusting the medical experts that my spine must be stabilised with rods as the only possible pathway to repair. The ongoing gentle interventions from all those flakes of kindness, that connected me with who I was, that encouraged me to persevere.

Love reinvigorates effort

Love is a powerful force – from others and from within. It unites our efforts. It evokes those around us to open the door to the aid they can offer. It enables us to be receptive of that support. Find moments to help others and yourself – practise being an angel.

In my journey, kindness arrived from so many unexpected places, at crucial times. One Thursday in the PAH GARU I woke up from a late afternoon nap to find a note beside my bed. It was from an occupational therapist at the hospital who'd heard of my condition via a mutual friend. She didn't know me but wanted to come by and offer encouragement and support. I was deeply touched by her attempted visit and kind note.

When we did catch up, she asked if I could help a student trainee with patient interactions, by being an informal mentor. A key skill for medical professionals is the ability to generate trust, comfort and rapport with their patients. I would be a dummy patient coaching the trainee in interactions to refine engagement techniques. The aim was to deepen understanding of patient issues to facilitate better diagnosis and treatment.

I leapt at the opportunity. It gave me something to participate in outside of my rehabilitation efforts. It was the tiniest puff that rekindled an ember of my identity as a mentor. Most importantly of all, it provided a little step back towards finding worth.

Love connects us with our identity, our embers of normality. It encourages us, replenishes energy and enhances our effort. It gives us focus. It forgives us our failures and picks us up for another try. Love and encouragement from family and friends about the improvements they saw and, importantly, the effort they saw me putting in, were crucial to sustaining energy and belief.

Before my accident I never would have known the uplifting power of the simple sentence, 'You are walking so much better than last time I saw you'. After hospital, I desperately tried to get back to participating in important parts of my life – reconnecting with those embers of normality – such as volunteering for my children's sporting teams.

I could not run, so I could not be the team's runner or boundary umpire like I had been before. I volunteered for the roles I could do, like being a ground marshal. Initially, this meant lurching around on my crutches and then wobbling around with my impacted gait without crutches. One of the dads at footy always took note of my progress, and never failed to encourage me. Every few weeks that I saw him he would pause, watch, then say something akin to, 'You are walking so much better than last time I saw you'. I felt immense pride hearing his praise. I would choke up inside, as I knew how hard-won those improvements were, and he seemed to know too. Most importantly, I gained immense energy and hope from those kind words.

I learned just how much strength love can give you, and how it helps you connect with your identity and belief. Love will come from many angels, in many guises – friends, family, strangers. It will get you through. Embrace it. Be present with those you love; be kind to those helping you. Your gratitude will allow you to see and embrace the positive aspects and learning moments throughout your journey of growth.

I was not prepared for the level of care I received from friends and strangers – people who gave willingly of themselves to improve my situation. People who went out of their way to provide extraordinary care, to send heartfelt messages of support. Those who shared stories of bravery with me in the hope of rekindling my belief. A series of small but powerful acts that touched and inspired me more than I could ever hope to convey.

Love reinvigorates effort. Learn to embrace and welcome it.

Become a fraction stronger

- Which friends and strangers have shown you care and kindness? Were any unexpected?
- Can you recall a piece of encouragement or praise you have received? How does it make you feel to remember and focus on what the person said?
- Can you identify any barriers, perhaps self-inflicted, that are stopping you from letting love in?
- Is there anyone in your life who deserves your love and care right now?
- When did you last perform an act of kindness? How good did it feel?

Part III

DEM-
ONS

The unknown, the uncertain, the despair, the fear.
The guilt of the impact on those we hold dear.
The loneliness, the failures,
Those opportunities we missed.
The jangling of nerves, tummy tight as a fist.
Numbing dislocation,
Yearning for completeness, for life as before.
You muster for the challenge, but deep does doubt gnaw.
Our demons they taunt us, they tease out the bleak.
So, reframe those dark thoughts,
Source motivation from demon-speak.

Bridge those tough moments, hunt for your purpose,
Inflame that faint light of hope.
Foster your resolve, to endure, to rise again above, cope.
It won't be easy, you'll need all your grit,
Foster pride in your best self as you unfold your own myth.

Inspired by confronting difficulty, and by Rūmī:
'Don't be satisfied with stories, how things have gone with others.
Unfold your own myth.'

Janine Shepherd AM was on her way to represent Australia at the 1988 Winter Olympics in Calgary as a cross-country skier. She identified deeply with her nickname – 'Janine the Machine' – driven by her Olympic dream. She was absolutely committed to being the best athlete she could be.

Janine was on a long training ride with her elite-athlete teammates. It was a perfect autumn day with a stunning summit finish in the scenic Blue Mountains, west of Sydney. As they reached the final section of the ride, Janine felt great. She was in her zone – finishing strong, outperforming. Winning.

Then she was struck by a speeding vehicle.

Janine almost died.

Janine broke her neck and back in six places. She fractured five left side ribs, her right arm and a collarbone. She broke bones in her feet. Her right side was ripped open; she sustained severe head injuries and internal injuries, and suffered massive blood loss. She was having – as she tells it – 'a really bad day'. In fact, she had a lot of bad days in a row.

But Janine lived.

She fought. She willed herself to do and be something special. She wrestled her way towards recovery and new meaning. Her journey generated meaning for me, and I hope it will stimulate meaning for you. But at that fragile point when hope was faint and energy was precious, it was all about finding meaning for her.

On that journey to new meaning, Janine tackled her demons.

In her first ten days, Janine recalls a spiritual feeling of drifting outside her body, watching from above. 'Why would I want to go back to a body that was so broken?' But her inner angel encouraged her: 'Come on, stay with me. This is our opportunity. We can do it. We can do it together.'

Janine took up her challenge. You can take up yours too.

She was told she would not walk again or have children. She did both.

But before those successes came hardship and despair. Janine was released from spinal care six months after her accident. As she prepared for discharge, the head nurse told Janine to be ready, because when she got home she would become depressed. 'See, it happens to everyone… you're going to get home and realise how different life is.' As Janine enjoyed those first precious moments released into the uplifting sunshine, she felt an enormous appreciation for life. 'How could I ever have taken this for granted?'

She felt joy and freedom.

Then she became depressed. She wanted her old life back, her old body back. She wanted to put her running shoes on and run out the door, to escape the awful circumstance she found herself in. She wanted to give up.

Janine persevered.

She found new meaning. She told herself, 'If I can't walk, then I will fly'. Janine flew. She wrote books, she spoke, she inspired.

You don't need to match all the incredible things that Janine has achieved. You just need to believe that when you get through the first tough moments, there will be better moments ahead. You can find those windows of hope like Janine did in her wheelchair when a passing plane triggered her urge to fly. You can find the moments to change your perspective. You can brighten the glow of possibility. You can refresh your identity, your sense of meaning. You can find your own version of flying.

Our emotions have a significant impact on how we feel and think. I don't know if it was because of my dad's periods of depression, but I always associated these negative voices and feelings with mental demons. That was how I thought of them when they pervaded my temper. Demons can impact our mood and belief, no matter our background or circumstances. They are not selective – they don't pick out just some of us. They don't hit only the sickest or most physically afflicted. They can impact elite athletes. They can affect us all.

When you are going through something difficult or uncertain, it is normal to have periods when you feel lost, desperate, scared and lonely. My experience is that you can contain and then reframe your demons with perspective.

Janine talks graciously about the positive influence of her spinal ward companion Maria, who had it incredibly tough, but kept smiling, never complained.

Appreciating that many people face deep and long challenges gives us perspective. It helps us not to dwell on our own circumstances.

Janine's drive to succeed helped her confront her demons, using them to inspire positive motivation. She pushed herself to walk and to fly. She achieved healing beyond her prognosis. And I bet she continues to push herself to beat that prognosis almost every single day.

Like Janine, I also confronted, contained and flipped my demons to become powerful motivation towards my recovery. So have billions of other people when facing their own adversity. And you can too.

Chapter 10
Reframing guilt

> 'How blunt are all the arrows of thy quiver in
> comparison with those of guilt.'
> – Robert Blair

My journey made me appreciate that energy and hope are symbiotic. When we find energy, we seek to focus it on something. Hope (or belief) is a productive avenue. As we establish hope, it gives us an incredible capability to summons that extra ounce of effort to generate, sustain or extend momentum. Condensing this, by combining the key thoughts I have shared before: Positive feedback reinvigorates effort and belief.

During my recovery, energy was perhaps even more precious than hope, especially in those difficult first weeks in hospital. I desperately wanted to apply my limited strength to looking and moving forward – I didn't want to waste it. I did my utmost to apply effort to what was helping me and avoid that which might hinder me. Practising gratitude really helped me concentrate my focus on the positives, and largely I felt I was successful.

However, our attention does not always meet our intention.

Charlie's 21 words

I was delivered some sharp perspective 21 months after my accident, when I was talking with a long-time friend, Kerry. My then 13-year-old son, Charlie, was with us. Driven by his school-teacher instincts, Kerry decided it would be more enlightening to get Charlie's version of events than mine. He asked Charlie to share his thoughts on the shock of that first week, and I was immensely proud of Charlie's mature reflections. But I was startled by his first 21 words. It wasn't 'I was so proud of the effort Dad put in'. It wasn't 'Dad had the most amazing positive attitude' or similar words that I had heard so regularly from others; the phrases I coveted as part of my recovery identity. I know Charlie is incredibly proud of my attitude and effort, but that wasn't what he remembers of the first week. He saw a dad who was totally different to the dad who had cheered him at cricket a few days before. A dad who was clearly struggling.

Charlie said:

'Dad, you looked so depressed. You were confused about how the accident happened. You were constantly apologising for letting us down.'

As I heard Charlie's unfiltered words, I immediately felt defensive and thought, 'Really?' Even today I genuinely still feel I reached 'acceptance' of my situation – and therefore was able to focus energy productively – much more quickly than is reflected in these 21 words. Hindsight does compress timeframes, and our own biases also filter how we perceive things.

If I step back from my feelings, I can see that Charlie's 21 words are a gift that perfectly captures the demons I was dealing with, especially with respect to my sense of identity. His words demonstrate what he witnessed in the short periods he was with me, measured against the dad he knew before.

Charlie was looking at me and seeing how far I had fallen. I was lying in bed with a different perspective: I was focused on how I could climb back up to stand beside him again.

This is one example of a consistent trend: that I would open windows to certain feelings at various phases of the journey depending on who I was with. With my family this centred on feelings of physical inadequacy and the future consequences of that. Issues that I recast as guilt, because of the financial and practical concerns that my injuries triggered. If I was with my cycling and hockey friends, it would be thinking or talking about my physical state that would trigger deep regret and temporary melancholy.

I know that I still open windows to my feelings today in certain settings, depending on where a conversation might go and which emotional trigger from my journey it might set off. Different feelings in different settings. Acknowledging how I am feeling and how my demons are being exposed is important. These emotions can have a significant negative impact on how I think and act, so if I can remain conscious of these feelings, I am more capable of managing them. If I can then successfully reframe them, they can provide a powerful source of motivation.

Charlie's 21 words capture the extent to which guilt was a significant demon for me. I felt deep shame that I had let my family down, that they would suffer the impact of my unlucky moment for the rest of my life. My thoughts ranged from, 'I was a great rider and safety conscious; how did this happen to me?' to, 'I do not want to be a burden to my family – how do I find a way to be useful?' It feels dramatic now – bordering on ridiculous – when I write or say it, but in those first hours, weeks and months I genuinely felt that their lives, as well as my own, might be ruined – and I was determined to do everything I could to reduce the tint of that taint.

When my loved ones were not visiting, I was utilising that guilt as constant motivation to progress. This was most of the time, of course, as I only saw my family for about 30 minutes per day – hence my perspective that I was largely successful at using my energy productively. But that is not what was playing out for the periods when they visited, which provided the window to Charlie's assessment. When my family saw me, I was wasting energy apologising profusely for a moment that could not be undone. 'I'm sorry, I'm so sorry', may have been uttered one hundred times in the first few days.

The phrase reflected not only that I was sorry for the current and future impacts to my family, but that I was feeling extremely sorry for myself – and petrified by my predicament.

Playing out my emotions

It didn't take many visits before Lucy acted. Another vital, gentle intervention. She delivered two important presents. I tried to feign (probably ineffectually) a hint of gratitude, despite feeling miffed by their arrival. As my mood settled, my perspective broadened. I came to embrace and appreciate them. They generated fun and proved influential in redirecting my energy away from guilt and towards productive action. As Terri Guillemets counsels: 'Guilt is always hungry, don't let it consume you'.

The first gift was the 'Sorry Button', a useless gadget that loops through a series of apologies when pressed. I suspect it was presented so that I could hear how irritating I sounded. It was a small act, but it made me more aware of how often I was expressing apology. It reminded me to apply my energy to the challenges ahead, rather than dwelling on the past. To focus on what I could control.

In the same visit, she also gave me a little flip book called *The Daily Mood*. I thought, 'What a load of crap!' Again, my response settled with time. During the next day, I asked for it to be passed to me and I discovered the first page was 'Addled', illustrated with a dazed green emoji. I couldn't recall ever using 'addled' in a sentence, but it grabbed my attention. It was such an apt representation of how I felt: confused about my future, dizzy from my head impact, and delirious from the effects of both pain medication and pain.

The Daily Mood was then perched on a hook on the wall at the foot of my bed. I thought I'd stick with Addled to start with, and we could see how I progressed. It was impossible for me to physically handle changing the mood myself, which worked out for the best. I could enjoy light-hearted moments with the nurses or other visitors, encouraging them to flip through the words and assign a mood of their choice to be on display for all to see. Some people loved that responsibility; others shied at it, which created an opportunity for them to ask for guidance – to ask how I felt. This made sure my emotions were regularly considered and addressed, if needed, by me and by my visitors.

Crazed, Focused and Wonky dominated. Borderline, Bouncy, Cantankerous, Chipper, Contemplative, Dreamlike, Fabulous, Fuzzy, Giddy, Hunky-Dory, Inspired, Listless, Maniacal, Mischievous, Rockin' and Wired all got decent display time, even if some of these were a little more upbeat than I felt. It was great to have the lighter moods showing!

The Daily Mood provided a visual reminder that I should acknowledge and address negative emotions AND celebrate more positive moments. The Sorry Button and *The Daily Mood* were enormously valuable additions to my hospital room, and to me.

Reframing your emotions

To break the cycle of guilt (and other negative emotions), the main tool I used was reframing. It is a method that I still regularly employ today, because guilt – or softer variants of it – continues to impact me. During my recovery I mostly reframed guilt into action. Rather than languish among my negative thoughts, I used them to find that extra piece of energy to sit up for longer, to move my feet, to do my lung exercises and protect myself from setbacks. To push through my discomfort.

I also used reframing to support my intent and attitude. I adopted positive mantras that I could attach to negative thoughts. These mantras continue to be important, because I expect it will be next to impossible for me to ever eradicate the sense of physical loss I have from my accident. I am reminded of my losses in every moment of every day, so I need to nurture my resilience.

My ongoing physical deficiencies mean I struggle to participate in even the simplest form of sport with my family, such as kicking a football. I can't cook with the gusto I used to – just lifting a full two-litre bottle of milk from the refrigerator fatigues me for a couple of seconds. Most noticeably, I struggle to keep up with my family when we walk together. This always triggers two immediate thoughts, in the same order. The negative one I can't help: 'I hate falling behind', then the reframing I have created to flip the emotion: 'At least I am walking, with some prospect of improvement'.

I cannot eliminate the guilt, so I use it as a flywheel for resilience as I strive to achieve my possible.

The word 'resilience' has its roots in the Latin verb *resilire*, meaning 'to jump back' or 'to recoil'. The Latin base of *resilire* is *salire*, a verb meaning 'to leap,' that is also part of the derivation of 'somersault'. I think visualising somersaulting provides a nice way to think of resilience: our ability to sustain forward momentum utilising the tumbles of life that put us in a spin! The turns aren't always in control, but by learning how to engage the power of the tumbling motion, we can steer ourselves. It's the centripetal force of our nature.

Now, I am not trying to convince you that bouncing back is easy. I know from my own experience that even once I did shift my moods, they could regress. What I'm suggesting is that if we embrace the gentle interventions and support around us, we can gain crucial perspective on our emotions. I know how important it was for me to reset by acknowledging how I felt. I would then seek opportunities to recall other moods or thoughts that would help me feel better.

If you can find a moment to ignite your sunnier thoughts, you might change your perspective for long enough to take positive action – and that provides scope to control or break the cycle.

Find goodness in guilt

Sometimes I challenge myself as to why I even refer to the feeling I associate with my constantly saying 'I'm sorry' as guilt. The crash was simply an unfortunate accident – I did not do anything wrong. In fact, I was doing something right. When I was cycling, I was looking after my health by doing something I loved, improving my physical fitness and refreshing my mind. That exercise aided my recovery. My fitness and leg strength was instrumental to the success of my rehabilitation.

I felt guilty because of the outcome, not the act, and for how that outcome created a gap between where I was and where I wanted to be – a shortfall in my sense of identity. Fortunately the guilt stemming from this drove positive behaviour.

Research by Rebecca Schaumberg and Francis J. Flynn confirms my experience.

Schaumberg and Flynn have performed studies that confirm that people with a higher propensity for experiencing guilt work harder, are more charitable, prove to be more capable leaders and are less prone to absenteeism. Their research suggests that we are less motivated than we might think by our own immediate interests. They found that the guilt people feel when they don't fulfil someone else's expectations provides a greater level of motivating power.

Flynn, a Professor of Organizational Behavior at Stanford University, says, 'Guilt is good. It actually has a lot in common with positive emotions.' Perhaps 'guilt is good' is a bit strong, and hopefully not as insidious as Gordon Gekko's 'greed is good'! I feel more comfortable to say there is power in guilt, used in a balanced way.

Rationally, I can see what Shaumberg and Flynn are saying about the motivating potential of guilt in response to external expectations. I struggle to see how this is sustainable, though. I think modern positive psychology coaches us not to focus on external expectations, as they drive disappointment. Internal expectations should matter far more to the balanced individual. Perhaps that is one way to digest this research – we have been more inclined to find motivation from external expectations than our internal ones, and this causes us to be stuck on our life treadmill, unwilling to establish what is our 'enough'. Putting us at risk of disappointment and burnout. It might also make it hard for us to draw boundaries around what we should feel responsible for.

I used expectations as a driver successfully. I generated this based on what I perceived others, including my family, might expect from me. I was projecting the moral identity I wanted them to see in me, and using it as a key motivating factor. Is that an internal or external driver? I believe it is the former that borrows from the motivating power of the external world. Does that make it balanced?

Rising above shame

I found sustaining balance difficult during my recovery, especially when it came to powerful feelings such as guilt and shame. Both emotions can deliver a debilitating blow to self-worth, if allowed to spiral unchecked. Guilt can sometimes transform into shame.

When I was first asked to talk publicly about my recovery, it was for the senior AFL squad at my boys' school. I was eager to do it, but I became inordinately self-conscious about the task. I wanted to be memorable (in a good way) and create a positive message these fine young men could share as motivation for their season ahead. As I worked on my presentation, I could never have expected they would embrace my speech's title – 'Stronger with them' – as their season motto: a message they had inscribed onto their training jerseys. To illustrate my surprise, it was perhaps a month after they gifted me a training jersey with 'Stronger with them' inscribed onto it that I realised that all the jerseys bore the same words. I had thought it was just a kind touch to personalise my jersey with my words!

The effort I put into the speech was a result of both believing I could make a positive difference, and shame. I didn't want to be ordinary. I didn't want to be bad, in case my boys were told by their school friends about it being boring, misdirected or soppy. I desperately wanted to avoid causing shame for them or myself.

Just as with the other challenges along the way, I succeeded by sourcing the right help. Friends referred me to a speaking coach. She told me to research other people who had been impacted by spinal cord injuries and start my talk with that. Somebody who the boys would connect with, so that they could contextualise my event. That led me to learn Alex McKinnon's story, which – as an AFL not NRL (National Rugby League) fan – I previously only knew as a few headlines on the news.

Alex was an Australian professional rugby league player before his devastating injury. He loved league. He practically grew up on the Aberdeen Tigers' footy field – which was named after his pop. He dreamt of being the first Tigers player to make it in the NRL. With his parents' support, Alex left his small home town to attend boarding school in the big smoke, Sydney. It was a massive change that took him out of his comfort zone and set him on a pathway to playing for the St George Dragons and then the Newcastle Knights. Alex was loving life and achieving his dreams.

In March 2014, playing his 49th NRL game, Alex's blossoming career was suddenly over. At just 23 years old, his life changed forever in a split second. Alex fractured two vertebrae in his neck playing for the Newcastle Knights against the Melbourne Storm.

Alex recalls the unbearable sense of shame he felt as he lay there. He was a big, hard, powerful player. He thought he was bulletproof. He remembers getting injured, thinking, 'This is pretty serious'. His immediate thoughts were of his family, of his partner Teigan. He felt like he wanted to be swallowed up – to disappear into the ground.

Alex identified as proud and strong, and in this moment he just felt weak. He hated that 20,000 people in the stadium were staring at him, that a huge TV audience was watching him. He could sense the coldness and silence of collective shock. All he wanted was to escape that focus – to be free from these witnesses to his moment of helplessness: 'Just pick me up. I don't care how you get me on the stretcher. Just get me out.'

He was an elite athlete. Everything was competitive. Everything was physical. In an instant that identity had been stripped from his grasp. Alex's neck injury left him an incomplete quadriplegic. There were so many things he could no longer do.

He was treated in the intensive care unit, then in a spinal cord injury ward for about six months. He then transferred to Burleigh Heads in Queensland to attend an intense rehabilitation program for about six months. He was among similarly impacted people, and he found he could cope with his challenges by training hard and doing his best to regain mobility. Striving to stand. Willing himself to walk.

There wasn't any miracle. His impact was severe and permanent.

Retuning to Newcastle after rehab was the hardest thing he had ever done, because he had never thought he would return home in a wheelchair. Those were his scariest days. He was rattled and couldn't even leave his house. He struggled with almost every activity – he remembers it took 30 minutes to plug an iPhone charger in.

'I just didn't feel adequate. I didn't feel. I just felt nothing.'

With time and support, he willed himself to try again. To reconnect with rehabilitation.

In November 2017, an Australian television program – *The Project* – televised a segment titled 'Love Conquers All', celebrating the story of Alex and Teigan, after Alex stood for 45 minutes during their wedding ceremony. As well as demonstrating the power of love, it was inspirational because to that point of his recovery, Alex's previous record for standing had been just 15 minutes.

Alex found the strength to stand because he was keeping a promise made to Teigan, his childhood sweetheart. It had been made two weeks after his injury, when he proposed. 'I will be standing beside you on our wedding day.' To rise on that special day, Alex had to find strength on so many days before that – to try, try and try again. To overcome heartache, disappointment and setbacks.

Alex's story reminds me that life is precious and fragile. But it also illustrates the power of effort. Alex trained for years to reach his goal of playing first-grade rugby league. Then he got flattened. He had to start again. So, he trained for more than three years to reach his goal of standing as he greeted his beautiful bride.

He achieved the exceptional with the support of many angels. He found a way to tackle and redirect that unbearable sense of shame caused by a shattered identity.

Guilt has been an ongoing emotion that has risen in me time and again during my recovery. I have been conscious of reframing it and using it to provide motivation to keep applying effort. On the long road to recovery from a significant injury, sometimes you need that little jolt to get you moving again – or to increase the urgency of your effort. In my experience, guilt can provide powerful motivation – provided it is acknowledged, managed and reframed.

Perhaps you already know the demon that helps you snap back towards your sense of identity, that makes you seek ways to close the gap between where you are and where you aspire to be. Utilise your desire to close the gap as motivation. To step into uncertainty. To make another effort, to liberate another possibility. To reframe those moments of guilt, or other powerful emotions, and turn them into positive action.

Motivate yourself by thinking about what you miss from your life 'before'. Use that feeling to drive you forward. But never lose sight of what you have.

I found it was important not to make false promises to myself that I would definitely make a full recovery, because I knew I might not. I treated the expectation gap as an aspiration.

Ultimately, the most valuable thing is how you feel about yourself; how you motivate yourself to improve. That relies on taking action to address or reframe negative emotions and managing your self-expectations.

You are resilient; it is your nature. Use it to bounce back from those bad turns.

Become a fraction stronger

- What is your current mood? Can you move forward by acknowledging it?
- What are the events or circumstances that often trigger guilt for you?
- When you sink into that guilt, do you feel any sparks of energy that might motivate you to work harder to turn things around?
- How might you reframe your guilt so it works for you rather than against you?
- Can you use humour to defuse your guilt and keep it from spiralling, as Lucy did with her gifts of the Sorry Button and *The Daily Mood*?
- Do you often feel your guilt morphing into shame? How might you prevent that from taking hold?

Chapter 11

Facing fear

'The most difficult thing is the decision to act,
the rest is merely tenacity.'
– Amelia Earhart

My fiercest demon was fear. From that moment of understeer on my cornering bike, I was confronted by wave upon wave of fear. It drove my instantaneous decision to select the least impactful crash alternative – the park ahead. It was with me during that doomed feeling of mounting the kerb, then hitting the pine barrier, knowing that one of those two events was going to fling me over my handlebars. The latter did it emphatically, catapulting me forward as my cycling shoes were wrenched from their cleats and my hands yanked from their grip on my brake levers. Fear soared with me for those split seconds in the air. Only my physical body fell back to earth with a thud. My fear remained elevated.

The collision with the ground whisked away my breath and delivered enormous pain. I had no ability or desire to move. I was significantly concerned about the extent of my injuries, although I can't recall ever thinking that this might relate to any current or future loss of movement in my legs. I am told that I noted I had pins and needles in my legs. I don't remember mentioning that, probably because I never thought anything sinister of it, especially once we tested that I could wriggle my toes. My cycling crew provided brilliant support, enabling me to remain relatively calm and persist until the ambulance arrived.

It was in the emergency department that my fear hit a completely new level. That jolt of terror as I was told that the crash impact had shot out a large piece of fractured vertebra, causing nerve damage and compressing my spinal cord. That they must operate and hope that the displaced bone fragment would be partially eased back out of spinal cord by that process.

What does that mean? How do I find a way to get around? What will life be like?

Experience had taught me that the only effective way to quell fear is to tackle it – so that was what I tried to do with all my courage. Face my fears. Perhaps I was aided by the extreme gravity of my situation, but it still took focus to get my mindset right, to find my brave face and confront fear. I did this by convincing myself that 'doing nothing' was simply not an option. Over those first few tormented hours, that was my entire focus. Facing my fears. Setting myself goals covering both attitude and outcomes. Committing myself to try with all my might, even if that meant failure.

Life is not about the fear in 'what might be'. It is about the 'what might be' in fear.

Just find a way to start

I am certain that this dedication to flipping fears into decisive action was a key mindset that supported my recovery. I used it to generate momentum towards my aspirations – to discover 'what might be' possible. This intent to act – not freeze – underpinned my conviction through a series of substantial hits of fear:

- Signing the declaration as they prepared me for surgery that acknowledged the risks to my eyesight presented by a five-hour, face-down operation. This was the first moment I recall any fear about the operation itself, because I was always proud of having incredible vision. I signed – I was not going to baulk at the opportunity to potentially get better, even with this peril. The operation was protecting more of my identity than it was threatening.
- Waking up from the operation and coming to terms with the extent of my immobility. My movement was limited and physically exhausting. I was on extensive pain medication, but any tiny movement still caused giant shots of pain. I experienced sharp nerve-related spasms caused by the ten deep insertions up my back where the rods and screws had been inserted.
- Standing for the first time with the help of two physiotherapists and a rollator frame, as I described in chapter 8. I was so desperately fearful of falling, of having a setback.
- 'Walking' from my bed to my doorway by leaning onto that rollator frame, supported by a physiotherapist on each side. Because my mind felt completely muddled about how to operate my legs or where my feet were, it haunted me for hours after the event.
- Experiencing complications with my catheter through that first week and failing to feel any bladder sensation once it was removed.
- Deciding on my hospital and other medical transitions as described in chapter 5.
- Being told I needed to be on the spinal unit waitlist as described in chapter 9.

• My first attempts to walk within the safety of the parallel bars, on the Tuesday of my second week. How deflating it was, with my leg control and sensory feedback issues. The sheer exhaustion walking just a few metres caused, with my dependency on my right hand to hold me up and help propel me forward.

I could list many more. The key point is that I faced these fears. I just put my blinkers on and found a way. I benefited from doing so – it liberated possibility.

Just don't fall

The scariest milestone of all was the standing x-ray, which was a hurdle I had to pass in that first week. It terrified me as an outcome and as a task. *What might it show? Will they operate again? Can I physically achieve it?*

For the days prior I was daunted by the challenge it would entail, knowing I would need to support my body weight with one arm for the duration of the x-ray. I had discovered that my legs had limited strength, no control and jerked wildly under strain. I was prohibited from using my left arm because of the injuries on that side of my body. I felt exhausted and weak. I feared that I would fall. I was terrified that any setback, such as an injury from falling, would shatter that faint hope of my best possible recovery.

My anxiety jumped to another level when they decided to x-ray me on Saturday, when Andy wasn't on duty. I considered the task next to impossible even with my trusted physio there to coach and encourage me. How was I going to get through this task without his help?

The process started with the normal palaver of getting all the layers off my legs, removing the resting night splint, unplugging and removing the intermittent pneumatic compression devices from my calves, peeling off the white compression socks, using a slide-sheet to roll and slide me onto the mobile bed, then wheeling me off to x-ray. I suffered a long and nerve-racking delay at x-ray due to an administrative error, before I was finally wheeled in and helped into position. No nurse or physio to support me, just the radiologists.

I held on with every fibre of my will. I would not allow my dreams to be shattered today. It was the fear of setbacks that enabled me to find the resolve to endure the task.

Don't give up

I chose the quote from Amelia Earhart over many other apt quotes that could start this chapter because of the tenacity element. My experience is that tackling fear does require all our grit. It is the willingness not just to step across the threshold into fear but to keep walking through it, even when there are setbacks and disappointments. Even when moments of hope prove to be false light and a new wave of fear hits us, we can always decide to get back up and apply effort to confront fear. It is a choice to act.

Even now, more than two years on, it is raw and emotional to reflect on each of the fears I faced, especially if I allow myself to dwell on them. I am sure that confirms I never had my fears under control, and I still don't. When they came, the only viable option I had was to muster whatever courage I could to face them, to keep facing them.

This choice to persist is captured with simplicity in the Japanese proverb, 'Fall down seven times, stand up eight'. And that is what I did. I kept willing myself to get up.

How did I do it? I obliged myself to trust Andy and the other experts supporting me. I thought about the fearful episodes in my past, like my first skiing holiday in New Zealand as a 23-year-old. I could not ski at all, and I was travelling with some very capable skiers. It was a trip in which I was constantly being pushed out of my comfort zone, which helped me improve faster. The scariest memory was not on the slopes – it was jumping from the 102-metre Pipeline bungee, which was the biggest adrenalin test of the era.

The drive out there was hairy enough. I was edgy with trepidation about the plunge ahead, but it was the condition of the road winding perilously around the steep mountainside that really unsettled me. Our bus was often sliding on the slippery, muddy surface, with the threat of a devastating accident if the driver could not keep to the narrow road. I found it a terrifying journey and I didn't have any significant fear of heights. Consequently, I have enormous respect for what Cara E. Yar Khan achieved during her epic descent into the Grand Canyon on horseback, which led to her saying, 'Life is really just a lesson in finding the balance between fear and courage'.

As we arrived at the Pipeline bridge, my nerves were at a peak, my stomach so tight and my skin crawling with anxiety and anticipation. Could I do it? Would I need to pull out of the jump due to fear? Avoidance was a clearly available option should I choose it.

Normally the best way through fear is to just do it, but in this case there was a lengthy queue. Rather than the delay exacerbating my fears, it gave me confidence. The operation worked like clockwork as one person after the other stepped up and jumped. I could use this sustained success to calm my nerves. Rather than be fearful of the challenges of the task, I simply formed a belief of how readily it could be done.

My bungee-jumping experience matches research about effective strategies to combat fear. I was watching people jump safely – sometimes happily – and then celebrate their sense of achievement from the adrenalin rush. It generated confidence in me. This is consistent with how repeatedly seeing other people climb without falling may begin to overwrite your negative association with heights. And the more you fly and land safely, the less dangerous flying is likely to feel. The experiences retrain your brain to develop a positive association with the thing that is triggering fear.

Facing your fears head on achieves this same effect. By combating fear one step at a time, you can increase self-confidence by achieving what once seemed impossible. Baulking at fear constrains you, while facing fear can liberate and transform. Janine Shepherd captured this concisely: 'Fear in itself isn't the problem, paralysis of fear is.'

Visualising success can deflate fear

During my recovery from the accident, I was not able to suppress or defeat the fear, so whenever it loomed I simply accosted it with belief and effort. I visualised that other people must have achieved these milestones before, otherwise they would not have progressed and the medical experts helping me would not be asking me to do it. I see this as reframing fear not as a wall in front of you, but as a tunnel that needs to be navigated to get to the light on the other side. The tunnel is far less ominous if you can visualise the light and the people before you who have successfully made the passage.

I faced my fears because I knew that by avoiding defeat, somewhere ahead I would find the chance to restock energy and belief, to refresh my vision of the possible. I put my blinkers on and focused on getting through this tough moment to get to better moments. No matter how frightening, progression was better than being where I was. It was always worthwhile to try.

In my experience, when we fail to confront our fears it embeds inertia or instigates flight. That sense of fear builds as you delay or dwell. That dreaded standing x-ray was never as bad as I was making it out to be in my head. Absolutely the physical challenge was exhausting, and I genuinely only just held on for the required duration using every ounce of my willpower. But the extrapolated thoughts such as 'If I fall,

I *will* have a setback, that *will* extinguish my slim chance of full recovery' and '*What if* the x-ray discovers complications and I need another operation?' were unhelpful extensions imagined from my fear. These negative thoughts were triggered by knowing the task was coming. The standing x-ray is only my most fearful memory because, as I waited for it to happen, I was fabricating fear rather than building belief.

When we are successful at addressing our fear, we gain momentum, and we change our perspectives. It doesn't matter if we only start small because even small successes will generate positive momentum. Even failures are positive, because we know we can start, we know we can try! And by trying, we give ourselves the opportunity for positive feedback – from ourselves or others – that will reinvigorate our effort.

Fear is an emotion that results from threat – perceived or real. This sense of peril directly and deeply stirs all the feelings connected with our identity, our values, our purpose. And there is so much power in our purpose. So, if we can flip that connection to become a positive force, we gain significant valuable motivation. We give ourselves the licence to achieve our best possible outcomes.

Find trust to face fear

Our family friend Tom faced down fear to liberate his recovery.

Tom was a gifted athlete, reaching Queensland Premier Rugby level in Brisbane. Talented at most ball sports, he was highly active with his rugby (union and touch), cricket, golf, tennis, gym and running.

At 24 years old, he was loving his role in sports marketing with the Brisbane Lions AFL team. It was his dream job. Life was great.

But Tom felt tired and groggy at times. He suffered bad migraines and motion sickness in vehicles and did not understand why. He put it down to mild anxiety due to the deadline and performance pressures of his exciting job.

One Friday morning at work, Tom suddenly felt sick and dazed as he stood up. He rushed to the toilets, where he passed out. He went home and slept for 18 hours, then rested almost all weekend. By Sunday afternoon he was finally starting to feel like himself, so he took a walk before joining his parents for dinner.

Tom seemed to have recovered from the bug that had toppled him. He wanted to get into a normal routine before starting the next work week. So, after dinner, he went for a run. About 7 km into his normal jogging loop, Tom woke up on the ground in a park with scratches on his hands and knees. He had no memory of passing out and no concept of how long he had been unconscious.

It was a traumatic event. Can you imagine the fear he felt? *What just happened? What does this mean?* He called his parents as he gingerly walked the 1 km to his apartment, where they met him to check him out. Collectively they decided he was still recovering and had overdone it with the run; he should keep his fluids up and get a good rest.

The next morning, Tom felt incredibly nauseous with his worst ever headache. It was so unbearable he decided to see his doctor, who sent him straight to the hospital emergency department. Initial tests explored heart issues as the most likely cause, finding nothing abnormal. An MRI was suggested and accepted – Tom was eager to find the cause.

About ten mins into that scan, Tom heard, 'Hey, we're just going to be a little longer – we want to have a closer look at your brain'. You can imagine how his anxiety ramped up. Alone, contained inside the MRI machine, Tom was suddenly confronted with thoughts like, 'Brain? I thought they were checking my heart? Oh geez, what the bloody hell is wrong with me?'

An hour after the MRI, Tom was told he could go home. He started to pack when a doctor came in and said, 'Tom, please stop packing and take a seat'. As he sat with his father waiting for an explanation of what they had found, Tom's stomach churned in fear. They learned Tom had syringomelia, an extremely rare condition where a cyst forms in the spinal cord. He would require the expertise of a neurosurgeon to see what could be done.

Tom had never been so scared. Within ten minutes of receiving the news, he was bawling his eyes out. He did not weep alone. Tom can only recall seeing his dad crying twice – when his own father died, and that day as he called his wife to explain the circumstances confronting their son.

In just a few days, Tom went from loving life to facing the fear of complex surgery. His cyst was at the top of the spinal cord bridging the C1 vertebra and brain stem, so there were significant risks of complications and side effects.

Tom and his dad had a difficult two-hour wait for the neurosurgeon. 'I've seen it in theory, but never in practice. But I can't see why I can't fix it.' Despite the uncertainties, the surgeon's demeanour calmed Tom. He shifted his mindset from fear by coaching himself: 'I don't really have an option here, so try and relax and let the experts do their jobs.'

The surgery was successful, but recovery was painful and challenging. Tom moved back home with his mum and dad for support – he was wheelchair-bound for a month, unable to drive for six months. He tackled the difficult task of recovery with the support of amazing physiotherapists. Walking was such a challenge it would take an hour to cover 500 metres – efforts that he was supported through by the company and love of his father.

In time, Tom made a successful physical recovery, almost back to full functionality.

Tom recalls that a powerful transition in his journey was when he flipped his thinking from what he had lost to what he could still have – to embrace life's second chance. With his parents' coaching, Tom stopped dwelling on what he could not do and focused on what he could do. They helped him break his post-surgery malaise and stimulated his drive to face his fears and find new worth.

Tom redirected his energy towards what he valued and how he could regain joy from those things. He could no longer play rugby at the Premier level, so he started to coach rugby at that level. He stepped into uncertainty to liberate new possibilities.

Tom faced fear with the help of his embers of normality – centred around the love of his family and the love of life. He came to realise he was extremely lucky to pass out as he did on that evening run. Finding the cyst when they did may have saved him from some form of spinal paralysation.

Tom's deep scare has left him with a much deeper gratitude for life, thanks to the expertise and care of others. He found new worth by facing fear. So can you.

Fear is perhaps the most primal of all emotions. It took hold from the moment I felt my bike understeer, propelling me towards peril. Fear continued to hit me in wave upon wave right through my early recovery.

I learned that the best way to tackle fear is to meet it head on. To get through each fearful moment – especially in the early days when I had no idea what my future might look like – I had to look my fears in the eyes. I had to find my brave face and take that first step into the unknown. I had to flip my fears into action.

And, once I had done that, I had to find the tenacity to keep moving through the fear – even as I stumbled and hit roadblocks. I had to trust the experts supporting me. I knew the only way out was through.

I believe if you can harness fear as motivation – as the trigger to take a step forward – you can tackle and overcome almost anything.

Build belief instead of fostering fear.

Become a fraction stronger

- What are some situations, memories or thoughts that trigger fear for you?
- Keeping just one of those fears in mind, can you visualise how you will feel once you face and conquer that fear?
- What is one step you could take today to reduce the power your fear has over you?
- Do some of your interactions exacerbate your fears?
- How can you change your perspective on those interactions, to recalibrate them, so that you can flip your fears to positive action?
- What is a fear you have confronted in the past? Does it still have a hold on you today? How do you feel about that?

Chapter 12

Dealing with despair

'There is hope after despair and many suns after darkness.'
– Rūmī

Despair is a debilitating demon. It descends uninvited, invading your thoughts and draining your energy. It permeates your sense of spirit just as a Dementor (from the *Harry Potter* series) might, sucking away your hopes and joy, pulling your fears and frailties into the vacuum.

Despair was one of my demons. I reeled under hits of bad news. I was rocked even by progress, because it typically came with a richer realisation of how tough the journey ahead would be. I often sensed my hopes shatter. The company of these troubles caused me to be emotionally fragile for much of my recovery. Despite my overarching sense of gratitude for my good fortune, old memories or new events still trigger these fragilities today.

My ebb of despair wasn't the shock news of my spinal cord injury. It wasn't the awful, muddled, lifeless sensation of my legs as I tried to stand and walk for the first time. It wasn't the weekend I spent hunched up in a world of pain because part of my medication had been omitted during my transition from RBWH to PAH. Those periods were bad, but none of them was the worst moment. That was triggered by nothing much at all – just the lonely thoughts of a severed identity. It was day 20, Friday 29 March 2019.

By that point, the core reason for me residing in the PAH GARU ward was physiotherapy support. My various discussions with medical experts had made it clear that early gains were the gateway to my hopes of a (near to) full recovery. I consistently heard that the first six months would yield nearly all my improvement. The prospect of any material gains after a year was low, and by two years almost non-existent. All advice came with the caveat 'but there is no clear guideline'.

I was desperate to maximise those early gains and my days revolved around rehabilitation. It became my interim identity, with every ounce of my energy and positivity focused on embracing what the physios and occupational therapists told me to do. It was my pathway towards finding worth.

I spent up to three hours each day in the physiotherapists' gym. I was allocated one hour of daily physiotherapy support, which regularly ended up being one on one attention because other patients did not show up. The physios allowed me to access their gym whenever it was open, provided I did not impact the treatment of other patients. This enabled me to return for a second session most days, to stretch and do the various exercise routines they had set for me. Practically every day I would be standing at the door to the gym at 9 a.m. when it opened, and again at 1 p.m. when it reopened after lunch. It became a standard joke across the ward that the first place to look for Mark was not his allocated bed, but the gym. If I wasn't in the gym I was eating or napping to recuperate, so that I could push myself again.

I was absolutely committed to recovery. The opportunity to invest time to get better and be expertly supported towards that goal, meant the world to me. I treasured the guidance of my physiotherapists.

However, the physio team did not work weekends and the gym facility was locked shut. Without an outlet for my improvement needs,

I was desperate not to be stuck all day in hospital – I desperately wanted to be home with my family. I could see no upside, and lots of downsides, to being in the hospital over the weekend.

I wasn't sufficiently well or mobile to safely reside at home. I could not shower or dress without help. I could not even stand upright without holding on to a bench-like structure with both hands. I could only hope to be allowed home for a few hours each day of that weekend.

I could use a wheelchair in our home once it had been carried up the stairs into our living area level by one of the family, but I hated the imposition of that. Even then, I would not be able to get from the sofa to the wheelchair to the toilet without help. There was no other means of getting around in our home – the rollator was too heavy and impractical to be an option.

I despised the thought of being an inconvenience to my family over their weekend. I felt I had caused enough disruption to their lives already. I felt shame about my invalid state.

A step change

I do not recall ever signalling how important getting home was to my physio Lucy, because I could not see a viable way for it to be achieved. I certainly didn't reveal my fears and frustrations about the prospect of being confined to a wheelchair. Perhaps physio Lucy sensed my yearning for release, but more likely her insight was self-initiated. I suspect training and experience drove her instinct that getting me home was important to both my physical and emotional health. To achieve that, she had to help me reach the next step of mobility.

At my Friday morning rehab session, Lucy tested me in the gym using a walking stick. It had to be held in my right hand, as my left wrist was not allowed to bear weight, and my left shoulder was supposed to minimise any weight bearing.

I could not balance for even a few metres across the gym. I tried again and was worse, with muscle fatigue further impacting my balance. I went back to my room. Devastated, lonely. I lay on my side in bed, knees tucked up to ease the pressure on my sore lower back. I hugged the pillow and sobbed. I wallowed in my woes. It was the longest and loudest cry of my journey, the only time I couldn't care who heard or what they thought. I curled up in a cocoon of sorrow on my bed, feeling desperately helpless and alone.

I could not face seeing anyone, so I was deliberately late for lunch. I could have put on my brave face so my table mates would be none the wiser about my concerns. But I didn't want to. I gave myself permission to feel sorry for myself for a while.

Once I knew the dining room would be clear, I got up and lunched in solitude – just me and my demon thoughts. How might I get home without being a burden? Then I sank lower: Do they even want me home? Of course they wanted me home, but once you lose perspective, your thoughts can cut deep.

I was doing my best to pacify my mood when two close friends paid a timely visit. Steve from the cycling crew and his lovely wife, Marina, are the sort of people that always find a smile and make you feel at ease. Their visit provided the perfect opportunity to reset – a gentle intervention to distract me from the moment. Their company enabled me to find some mental balance amidst the isolation of my physical imbalance. It led me back to a happier place. I reconnected with my embers of normality.

We were approaching our farewells when physio Lucy suddenly appeared, beckoning me with a broad smile and potential solution. 'Can you come with me, Mark?' She was bearing a few different crutches for me to try. I said my goodbyes and went into the gym, where Lucy trained me in how to use one normal Canadian crutch and one gutter crutch. The padded arm-piece of the gutter crutch was ideal to reduce force through my left side. It protected my left wrist from any weight bearing. I was slightly wobbly and needed to be very careful turning, but I could navigate a few metres without danger.

Lucy cleared me to use these crutches for short distances at home, provided a wheelchair was used if I ventured outside. I was delighted with my newfound freedom and mobility. It liberated me physically and emotionally. It was an example of the Kurdish proverb, 'Stairs are climbed step by step'.

Lucy provided an important step change towards recovery, when someone with a more conservative viewpoint could have decided that even employing the gutter crutch was not appropriate given my fractured scapula. Perhaps it helped that just six months before, Cooper Cronk had played and won an NRL Grand Final with the same shoulder injury!

Physio Lucy had the courage to identify and deliver a solution that brought more benefit than risk. Her resourcefulness lifted me from despair and her actions provided important motivation I could revisit: 'I don't want to drift back to that ditch of despair – I want to feel like my recovered self will feel.' I found solace in that mental space many times over the weeks and months ahead.

Despair is contrary

In chapter 9, I shared the depth of my day nine devastation, when PAH Spinal told me I needed to be placed on their waitlist. Their words shredded my hopes of making rapid progress towards a miraculous recovery. It was nurse Nicole's timely investment of kindness that Monday morning that eased me from that moment, stopping it from cutting much more deeply. She granted me the gift of perspective.

Twenty-one days after Nicole picked me up and encouraged me to look forward, that same PAH Spinal team rocked me to despair again when they took me off their waitlist. There was no nurse Nicole standing by to console me as I wept softly in self-pity once they had left.

I suspect that may seem very strange to you, the contrariness of my despair – that three weeks earlier I had been wailing because I was waitlisted, and then I was lamenting because I was not. If you are wondering why the impact of them removing me was almost as deflating as when they put me on their waitlist, the explanation has two parts.

Firstly, in those 21 days I had gained a much deeper appreciation of just how long and difficult my journey back towards physical recovery would be. One of my potential avenues for sustaining or possibly accelerating my improvement was now shut down. I was borderline for receiving PAH Spinal's help but just on the wrong side of that cut-off. That was both good and bad news. If I had been admitted, I would have received a broader range of assistance. Now I had to navigate those pathways through uncertainty myself, including securing my treatment options beyond in-hospital care.

The bigger blow came from me deciding that this was my golden opportunity to ask the hard questions about their views of my prospects. It was their last assessment (of four) and a chance to test and address assumptions about my progress and my goals. I decided I was going to ask all my bravest questions, no matter how much I might not enjoy their answers. I was deeply impacted when those answers confirmed outcomes I had already accepted as likely but desperately didn't want to be 'true'. Outcomes such as wearing an ankle foot orthosis (AFO) all my life, having no prospect of a full recovery or the ability to run again.

There were tears when they left, again. Only soft ones, because I knew these answers, I just didn't want to hear them.

I knew their answers were just one set of perspectives, just one version of the array of potential outcomes. I knew the discussion didn't change my prospects of running, or of over-performing the prognosis in other ways. It impacted me because it changed how hopeful I felt about those things, and hope is a valuable wand to ward off despair.

The discussion hurt, but it didn't take long before I picked myself up by thinking, 'Enough! I want to feel like recovered Mark will feel.' I found solace in activity and music in the gym, taking one small step forward from that grip of despair. Effort and attitude were invaluable tools to help me progress, one step at a time.

Now I just want to digress for a minute to clarify that in my mind there is a massive difference between accepting that something is likely and accepting that it will happen. This moment of despair came from PAH Spinal and I seeing the same outcomes as likely, not inevitable. Because none of us could predict what would happen.

Even in the deeper moments of despair like this one, I don't think I ever totally gave up on the possibility of the exceptional outcome that I was pursuing. I was feeling low because I had discovered my outcomes might be harder to attain than I wanted them to be, and more akin to where they were proving to be. This is just perspective of course! Nothing had changed – my physical condition was not suddenly worsened by this matching of my maturing internal perspectives with an external view.

Step out of despair

Despair can consume us. It can hold us in the moment and stop us tackling uncertainty. It narrows our perspectives and stops us from seeing the range of possibilities. It mires us in the mud of our current situation.

Despair is only an internalised emotion. It seeks to draw us into that 'why me', 'woe is me' mentality. As with all of our demons, we can choose how we deal with despair. It can consume our energy, and exhaust and confuse our mindset. Or we can find the message, the trigger, the feeling that helps us use it as positive motivation to drive us towards our goals – to adopt the Benjamin Disraeli mindset that 'There is no education like adversity'.

Which option do you like the sound of? I kept encouraging myself towards the latter, often with the help of important interventions.

My process from despair to balance typically went like this:

1. Allow a short wallow. Let it out.
2. Acknowledge this is how I feel *at this point in time.*
3. I could never remember all the Cognitive Behavioural Therapy I learned 15 years ago so I fumbled through my own version of 'It is just your emotions distorting perspectives'.
4. Hang in there. Tell myself it can and will pass.
5. Allow myself some time to reset, including cancelling or deferring activities.
6. Then, at the first opportunity to progress, I repeated this loop:

    a. At the slightest hint of the despair easing, I would take the next available opportunity to do something. Anything.
    b. I started with small activities. Typically exercise. Or cooking. Something I enjoy that connects to my identity.
    c. Then I would seek out or embrace something bigger to do. Reach out to someone, or accept to see someone. Discuss something other than my woes. Touch and rekindle my embers. Rekindle my identity.

I used this strategy when I needed to get back up after the PAH Spinal Unit took me off their waitlist. I used it regularly during my recovery, including one important day about 16 months after my injury.

That morning, I had a phone discussion that destabilised me. I was scared again. I felt flat, I felt lost. I had to cancel a coffee catch-up with a friend who was always supportive, but the discussion would have been geared heavily towards checking in on personal wellbeing. I could not deal with those emotions at that moment. I would have choked up about my current fears. I did not think that would help me.

I took some time at home. I focused on my rehabilitation exercises, activity I could do that helped move me from my moody moment. Then I got a surprise call from another friend seeing if I could meet him for lunch. I was feeling brighter, and I wanted that brightness to strengthen. I knew that lunch with this friend would be full of intellectual, stimulating conversation about global economics and business leadership issues. It would ignite embers of normality for me. I took up the invitation. The company was great. My opinions and thoughts were valued. I felt better, more capable.

Later, out of the blue that evening, an angel emailed me – a negotiation coach from a long time ago. We'd stayed in regular contact, and I considered him both a mentor and friend. He wanted to explore a part-time opportunity. Something flexible that might fit better with my physical capability than what I had tried to achieve during the last six months. Something that alleviated the fears triggered by that morning call. I was receptive to it because of the momentum I had built during the day.

Is this helping or harming?

Around that time, I became familiar with Lucy Hone's story of dealing with despair. As I listened to her speak, I could see how I had used some of her strategies without understanding the science behind what I was doing.

Lucy is a resilience researcher who completed her doctorate studies at the University of Pennsylvania before commencing her own research in Christchurch, New Zealand. Lucy put her study on hold to focus on helping the Christchurch community deal with the destruction resulting from the devastating earthquake of February 2011, which ruined 3500 homes, injured 6659 people and took the lives of 185. Dealing with the extensive impacts to her community put her significant expertise to good use, helping many people and businesses deal with the unprecedented upheaval to their lives and welfare.

Then in 2014, Lucy's 12-year-old daughter, plus a dear friend and that friend's daughter, were killed in a horrific car crash. Suddenly Lucy was the one upheaved, and in the worst possible manner: losing a child. Lucy found herself on the end of the expert advice, and she realised that some of the well-meaning guidance she had been giving needed a stronger linkage to hope. Her difficult personal journey confirmed what she knew from the research:

- That you can rise up from adversity.
- That there are strategies that work.
- That it is utterly possible to make yourself think and act in certain ways that help you navigate tough times.

Lucy shared three secrets of resilient people that resonated for me. Perhaps they resonate for you too:

1. Understand that suffering is part of life.
2. Tune in to the good.
3. Ask yourself, 'Is this helping or harming me?'

When I watched Lucy talk, I could see how her messages aligned with the actions I had unconsciously taken in my journey. I had understood that I was not alone in suffering – in fact I had visualised people who achieved recoveries from more difficult positions to encourage myself it could be done, that I wasn't alone in facing a challenge. I practised positivity by trying to find the hope and good in my situation. Whenever possible, I tried to focus my energy on the actions that were helping me progress, rather than hindering myself by languishing in loss.

I am convinced Lucy's three secrets of resilient people are powerful behaviours to support dealing with despair and disruption.

Many times during my recovery, despair caused my vision to cloud and my motivation to plummet. At times it caused me to feel so lonely and despondent I began losing my grip on reality.

As you have read throughout this book, I took any opportunity to move forward and make progress. But despair is a sneaky demon – it would arrive in an instant, invading my thoughts and playing on my fears and fragility.

Despite it all, I was eventually able to get up and get going again after each desperate moment. I believe this is due to two things: my angels helping me defuse those moments of paralysis that despair can bring, and my determination to find a way through. To help myself.

I know that in the darkest moments, it can be difficult to take the action you know will move you forward. This is when you must let your angels find you. Respond to their love and be grateful for it. Lean on others when you can't find hope yourself.

You may never eliminate the cycles of despair completely. I certainly haven't. But in time, you will find you can break out easier, or sink less deeply in the first place.

Never forget you are a powerful angel, too. You have the power to help yourself and others through.

Become a fraction stronger

- Thinking about a time when you have felt despair, what do you think it was triggered by?
- What is the best way you know to help yourself through desperate moments?
- Can you think of anyone in your circle of friends and acquaintances who has worked through times of deep despair? Can you take inspiration from their story?
- Who are the angels surrounding you with the power to pull you out of the depths of despair?

Chapter 13

Finding worth

'You can't go back and change the beginning,
but you can start where you are and change the ending.'
– C.S. Lewis

In chapter 4 I introduced Morgan Housel. His words – 'You don't need tremendous force to create tremendous results' – resonate because that is exactly how I felt (and continue to feel) about my recovery. I was relentless. I consistently aimed for the next small gain that kept me on track towards my aspirational goals. I put aside the inhibitions of pride and sourced all the help I could find. These interventions amplified the impact of my efforts.

I was prepared to do the little, hard things over and over and let them accumulate. I welcomed any assistance with the rebuilding of my identity. These acts and attitudes helped me at the time, and they created embers I will rely on forever.

I focused on the processes of trying, of listening, of seeking and welcoming help. If I did that, I felt the outcome would be more capable of looking after itself. I was absolutely committed to the physical recovery process, and I wanted that process to propel me to self-worth.

Just like Michael Lewis says in *Moneyball*, one of my favourite books (and films): 'This is a process. It's a process, it's a process.'

Small acts compound

I was consistently told that my scope for physical improvement would wane quickly with time. I accepted that the opportunity to make a difference was greatest in the first three to six months. I was desperate to grasp as much of that as possible, by making progress and avoiding setbacks. My early gains would provide a launching pad for a better overall recovery.

I craved all potential gains, no matter how small or when they presented. I would tell myself and others, 'I know the gains will become increasingly marginal, but I intend to live another 30 years, so the payback on any gains is huge'.

I used this saying to encourage myself that no matter how scary or tough some of my exercises might be, no matter how much energy (emotional and physical) they absorbed, all the effort I was investing into rehabilitation would accumulate and compound.

All those tiny gains to make myself a fraction stronger would pay off for a better quality of physical life in the future, and a better physical life gave me a broader scope of possibility for rebuilding my family and work identity. It was my rhythm for finding worth.

Sure, I hoped for a miracle, especially in the beginning. But that never distracted me from putting in the effort to tackle the reality of my circumstances. Hard work plus help was my plan A. If a better, easier plan popped up then happy days, but I wasn't going to waste energy looking for it.

My planning centred on sustaining a resolute attitude rather than being rigid on outcomes. This meant I was more flexible and capable of navigating uncertainty. I firmly believe many roads can lead to success and the key is a balance between persevering and adapting.

Be inventive

Inventions contributed significantly to me closing the gap towards my 'worthiness'. There was physio Lucy with the mixed pair of crutches that lifted me from my lowest point of despair. There was my proud modification of the backless Singapore Airlines slippers, which I described in chapter 7.

In hospital I had a 'dressing assist hook', which I used to pick my shoes up off the floor so I could put them on. I couldn't reach them otherwise. That stick was important for protecting self-worth, including when I used it to lasso the rollator back towards me when the nurses had moved it away from the bed. I couldn't stand up without it and I was impatient for independence; being able to help myself helped reinforce my worth.

Once I got home from hospital, I needed to work out ways to get up and down our stairs safely while holding my crutches. Our handrail is on the left while ascending. My left arm was my protected arm (it couldn't bear any weight), so I had to work out how to carry my crutches in that hand while using the right (across my body) to help haul myself up the stairs, given my legs were not strong enough to do the task alone. I needed to establish a way to get safely in and out of my pool to do my hydrotherapy routine. I needed to navigate our laundry steps safely. Their lack of handrail made it a scary experience, but one I learned to navigate by holding onto the door frame, then the clothesline. It allowed me to contribute to the family by slowly and painfully hanging out washing. I couldn't carry the washing basket, I had to slide it along the floor to the doorway first. These were some of my small acts on the pathway to finding my worth.

Establish necessity

During my final school year my family started watching a television series titled *Bush Tucker Man*. It ticked three popular criteria in our house: documentary, nature, and (of course) it was on the ABC. It featured Major Les Hiddins AM, a war veteran who had gleaned a comprehensive knowledge of native food sources from Indigenous communities while authoring the Australian Army's military survival manual.

The show filmed Major Les driving around the harshest, most remote regions of northern Australia, uncovering and eating unlikely meals. I loved it for the way it shared stunning Australian landscapes, interesting history and First Nations traditions.

The show was such a surprise success that Major Les retired from the Army and carved a career from his survival expertise. One avenue of this was a series of advertising endorsements. My favourite ad featured Les and a 'Coolgardie safe' – the 1890s invention that utilised evaporation of water from hessian cloth walls to cool food in the sweltering hot Western Australian goldfields. The advertisement's tagline of 'Necessity is the mother of invention' stuck with me and my friends. It was generously repeated in a wide range of circumstances. Turn up at a party without a stubby holder? No problem, make a temporary one out of cardboard and state 'Necessity is the mother of invention'.

Jokes aside, I think this mindset is massively influential: from applying effort, to dealing with your demons, to liberating possibility and exploring pathways. It overlays a powerful 'can-do' attitude onto a resolute sense of 'why'. Rather than letting your circumstances overwhelm you, you dig deep for resolve and identify ways to start, to persist and to overcome challenges. It is a commitment to stay the course no matter the state of the road.

I am convinced this mindset helped me find my worth during my recovery.

Did I have a genuine necessity to get better? Not really. It would have been a far easier road to contest my circumstances with less conviction.

My resolve drove me down the harder path. I made it a necessity. I chose aspirational goals that reflected my sense of identity. I manufactured the willpower to give this recovery my absolute best shot. I established self-expectations about the standards that my attitude must reach, based on my sense of purpose. I did all these things because in my mind it was the only pathway that led to self-worth, as I visualised that abstraction during the initial phase of my recovery.

Keep it positive

Giving it my 'best shot' became my interim identity. Consequently, for a long period my perception of self-worth was concentrated on my attitude and ability to maximise physical gains.

When you are desperate to find worth in a narrow way, as I was, it can be a tightrope traversing self-doubt and regret. I was prone to self-criticism if I got distracted by the events of a day and missed a home rehabilitation session. I had no catch-up capacity – in the evenings I had inadequate strength and my pain was too intrusive to do any activity to the quality required. I had to cut myself some slack. I acknowledged that accumulating improvement was about getting most of the days right. I didn't need to get every day right.

There were moments of regret too. When I was first introduced to Leanne for that crucial physiotherapy intervention I wondered 'Why didn't this happen earlier?' and 'If only I could have more sessions with her'. But Leanne's intervention may never have been as impactful if I hadn't recovered my strength to a sufficient level when we met.

I learned it is crucial that we take the opportunities when they arise, rather than lament when they didn't.

From early 2020 – around ten months after the accident – I started juggling part-time work and rehabilitation, which proved a recipe for self-doubt. It felt like both activities were compromised. I was struggling to have the influence in my work that I wanted, and I felt that I was compromising my longer-term health prospects because of the extent to which part-time work was fatiguing me. Eventually this came to a head, with physical complications meaning I had to step back and reassess my work capabilities. It was a key development that in time would cause me to reassess my pathway to self-worth. I reached a point where it became clear that pushing myself harder for each progressively small gain might be sensible for my physical improvement, but it wasn't going to work for mental wellbeing or feelings about my intellectual worth. This disillusionment opened my mind to exploring new pathways.

Embrace interventions

That expression I learned from Major Les, 'Necessity is the mother of invention', is said to be adapted from the Plato proverb 'Our need will be the real creator'. I am going to mould the expression further, broadening it to 'Necessity is the mother of *inter*vention'.

I am many fractions stronger for all the gentle interventions that helped me pursue my goals. I identified that it was a necessity for me to reach out often and extensively for help. Perhaps it took me a week to genuinely start doing so, when my 'cry for help' email to Bicycle Queensland (BQ) exposed both my need and fragility. I didn't know it at the time, but this act of acknowledging my fears and uncertainties was a crucial step forward. BQ's compassionate response provided an immediate positive experience of how powerful reaching out can be.

It encouraged me to keep seeking and welcoming help. All the consequent small interventions compounded to create my successful recovery.

There was the crucial intervention from physio Andy in that first week, when he lowered my expectations and encouraged my resolve. 'For the next year or beyond, recovery is your full-time job. Focus all your energy on it. And you will need ongoing maintenance for the rest of your life. Prepare for it'. While it initially shocked me, and I was determined to find a way to outperform his assessment, I embraced the intent. This was a marathon not a sprint, but even in a long-distance race you need to be able to sprint at times to make sure you are well-positioned.

There were many other interventions, including ones I have shared so far, such as those from my wife Lucy (particularly when she advised against googling my injuries and gifted me the Sorry Button), nurse Nicole and physio Leanne. I am also incredibly grateful for the social workers at PAH GARU (plus Dr Madi and physio Lucy) who drove my National Disability Insurance Scheme (NDIS) application. Without their determination I would have readily dismissed it, and my recovery and sense of self-worth would not be remotely close to where it is today.

My wife aside, it was Brian who was most influential in the key self-worth moments for my recovery. Before my injury he was an occasional school acquaintance. From the belief he provided for me in hospital, to the way he checked on me and offered to be an exercise buddy, all the way to how he helped me to transform my self-worth (which I will cover in the next, final chapter), Brian became my guardian angel. I believe he did this both because of his own journey and because of the example his own father, Gavin, had provided for him. I consider their stories and how they impacted me as a series of small acts that cascaded into tremendous results.

Reach for your dreams

Gavin was a Toowoomba primary school boy when his dad took him to Jack Evans' Porpoise Pool at Snapper Rocks, Gold Coast, Queensland. By chance the New South Wales diving troupe – a touring group showcasing some of Australia's best divers – was doing an exhibition that day. It captivated Gavin, and years later he could still recall the whole show from first to last dive. Back in Toowoomba he started recreating what he saw. He spent hours diving off the springboard at the local pool, staying under the water as he kicked his way back to the ledge (Gavin couldn't swim). At home, he'd pile up the lawn clippings and jump off the roof of their house, somersaulting and landing on his feet in the cut grass.

In November 1964, when Gavin was 15, he attended a Louis Armstrong concert in Brisbane and took the chance while he was in the big smoke to visit Brisbane's Centenary Pool. He was messing about on the diving boards when he was spotted by Olympian Graham Deuble, who encouraged Gavin to trial the sport. Gavin leapt at the possibility – his passion for football had been snatched away from him by juvenile osteoporosis and he hated not being able to participate in sport. The invitation meant much more than just a chance to try – Gavin felt he was being offered a pathway to finding worth. To compete again as he had loved doing when playing football.

Gavin gave up school early and moved to Brisbane, residing in a boarding house and working odd jobs as he pursued his diving passion. In winter, he would hitchhike to Sydney every few months for additional coaching, as Sydney had the benefit of heated diving pools, which Brisbane did not.

In 1968 Gavin completed a clean sweep of the Queensland men's open diving championships. Two seconds and one third at the Australian titles qualified Gavin for the 1968 Summer Olympics in Mexico City, but his dream of competing was cut away, with the budget constraining selection to one diver per event.

Then, in December 1968, Gavin suffered a terrible car accident in which his knees were crushed under the dashboard. After six weeks of bedridden care in hospital, he was told by the specialist that he would never fully recover. His knees would suffer permanent stiffness. He would walk with pain and gait deficiencies. Gavin was shattered – just months before, he had been within a splash of his Olympic dream. But he wasn't prepared to give up. 'There must be another way', he thought.

The orthopaedic surgeon who had delivered the shocking news was Dr Tony Blue. 'I know that name', Gavin thought. He remembered that a runner named Tony Blue had competed at the 1960 Summer Olympics in Rome, where his coach Graham had competed in diving. The next day, when Dr Blue arrived, Gavin was compelled to try the connection – there was nothing to lose. 'Did you compete in Rome? Do you know my diving coach, Graham Deuble?'

It opened a door to build rapport. Dr Blue said, 'There is one thing we could try, but it will be extremely tough and only has a slim hope of success'. Gavin was transferred to hospital, where he underwent six weeks of intense rehabilitation. He had long periods of treatment during which he was covered in ice up to his hips. He was suspended in water so he could regain the range of movement in his legs without gravity's load. He revelled in the challenge and was put on a pathway towards full recovery by the program that Dr Blue facilitated.

Gavin resumed competitive diving even though his injuries constrained him to performing only straight leg dives. He won the 1970 Queensland state diving titles and finished fourth in that year's Commonwealth Games trials. By 1972 he had regained his range of movement and was back in contention for his Olympic dream, before another tragedy. Just four days before the selection trials, Gavin was struck by a negligent car crossing Brisbane's George Street. Then, in 1973, another severe car crash left him with pins in his hips and on crutches. He was desperate to get home to his wife Angela and three-year-old boy, Brian. Gavin slowly fought his way back to physical health with Angela supporting him, hauling him onto his crutches so he could get around.

The 1973 injury caused Gavin to reassess his priorities. Family was integral to his self-identity. He completed his high school certificate as a mature age student and enjoyed a successful teaching career, helping others find worth. He maintained an interest in diving. In 1994, Gavin competed at the World Masters Games, securing a gold and a silver medal.

Gavin's determination to keep fighting back, to explore possibility and find his worth, had an impact on his children, moulding Brian into the fine man he is. When Brian was hit by a truck – a story I shared in chapter 6 of this book – Gavin supported Brian to recover and regain his worth. Then Brian's interventions helped me find my worth. A series of small actions accumulated to help change the trajectory of my life.

Reframing my worth

I consider the battle to find worth a bit different to the battles with my other demons. Despair, fear and guilt tend to be flash fires. An external spark or internal thought triggers an unhappy ember inside me to flare, causing flames that I need to tackle or control.

Finding worth was more like a constant low rumble. It was a sustained, slow burn that motivated me to pursue that abstraction I had of my identity. A fire inside me driving me to meet my self-expectations and close the physical gap, with the plan that in doing so

I would rebuild all the elements of my identity that had been shattered by the impact of my accident.

During 2020 I worked out that the physical gap was never going to completely close, despite my best intentions. I would have deficiencies for life, and it would take sustained effort not to regress. I don't think this had any genuine negative impact on me, as I had been prepared for this since the start. While I yearned for a full physical recovery, I knew that in aiming for that aspirational outcome I was likely to fall short. It is exactly like the Michelangelo quote I shared in the introduction: 'The greatest danger for most of us is not that our aim is too high and we miss it, but that it is too low and we reach it.'

The greater issue that I was coming to appreciate was that the shortfall in my physical recovery was deeply connected to my working capacity. It therefore had much wider implications for my sense of self-worth than I hoped. Only by reaching the level of physical recovery that enabled me to restart working did I get to see this new challenge. It is a bit like mountaineering – when you struggle to hike to the top of what you believe is the summit, only to see that there is another climb ahead that has only just become visible.

It was a good problem to have. Without the learnings I have shared in this book, I never would have achieved the level of physical recovery that I reached, and this new identity shortfall may not have impacted me in the way that it did. Good or not, it was a problem that I had to face.

The accumulation of continuous tiny improvements supported my self-worth. I was determined to take hold of any opportunity for physical gains because I knew every milestone reached would help me rebuild my sense of self.

Doing the best I could became my new identity. I gained worth by making sure my attitude and effort were both consistently applied towards my vision of recovery. But I cut myself some slack, too, understanding that seeking perfection every day was not conducive to a positive mindset.

Many times, it was angels who lifted me and stoked my embers. Interventions that helped me find a reason to keep pushing myself towards self-worth.

In time, I discovered that to become a fraction stronger, I needed to force myself into uncertainty once more. Just as the quote at the beginning of the chapter guides us – we can always begin again.

Become a fraction stronger

- Have you experienced an event or circumstance that has rocked your self-worth?
- What aspects of your identity did this threaten?
- What are some small goals or milestones you could work towards to regain your sense of self?

Now a fraction stronger

'We are all capable of extraordinary things when we loosen
our grip on how we think our life is supposed to look.'
– Janine Shepherd

My accident dislocated my physical, family and work identities.
Despite my best intentions, it was always going to take time to establish
new meaning from what I could do, and move on from what I couldn't
do. An identity accumulated over a long time is not quickly released.

The decision in 2020 to remove the fixation rods from my back
triggered a series of events that challenged me to practise many of the
lessons of this book again, shifting my focus more firmly onto what
I could do.

I was fortunate that my operation went ahead on 11 March
2020, just as the first wave of the COVID-19 pandemic was taking
hold in Australia. However, I greatly underestimated how much this
operation would impact me. I saw it as a mild event compared to
what I had been through a year before, which it was, but it was still
a significant invasion into my back muscles to extract the rods and
screws. Additionally, an infection inside one of the surgical incisions
complicated the recovery process.

Consequently, March to June 2020 ended up being a frustrating period. I was struggling to have the influence I wanted on a work project and was feeling mentally lost on top of being physically sore. Having my body and identity feeling battered again started to wear me down, so I applied what I had successfully done before: I set achievable goals to regain momentum. As I have said many times: positive feedback reinvigorates effort and belief.

These goals became the moments that opened the door for me to find new meaning.

Moments create moments

One of my key moments of becoming a fraction stronger stemmed from jogging a lap of an oval. I'd been building up to it for about nine months, doing a series of pre-running drills that a physiotherapist had provided me. Heel flicks, high knees, mini lunge steps, tippy-toe walking – just doing ten metres of each at a time. It drained me but I persevered. I did it at least four times each week, and often daily. I yearned for that milestone: running. It was part of my identity.

The rods that were screwed into my vertebrae created a jarring that inflamed my back during any movement, including walking. I felt severe discomfort during and after any attempts at jogging. So I deferred my goal of attempting to run until after my metalwork was removed.

I felt confident that I could probably jog 40 metres, but I knew I would tire quickly beyond that. I didn't know how long I would be able to persist for, and I was nervous about how fatigue would impact my form and balance. I didn't want to create a setback by tripping or inflaming some other part of my body.

I elected to face the fear. I set a date and decided that I would throw myself into uncertainty by attempting to run a full lap of the oval. A moment back in April 2019, when I resolved to defy the PAH Spinal Unit's prognosis, finally bloomed in June 2020.

The actual jogging event triggered a mixture of emotions. Inspiration, relief, realisation and pride were perhaps the top four. Inspiration because of the reward I felt having achieved a stretch target I'd set as an act of defiance a year before – it reinforced that sense of being able to achieve exceptional things if I applied myself. Relief because I could do it, and all the effort had been worth it – my hope hadn't been misplaced. Realisation of just how poor my running capability was, how my legs only had the strength for jogging 25 metres or so and the other 375 metres around the oval had barely been a shuffle. I still had so much improvement to strive for. And I was proud for having a crack, proud that I'd set a tough target and chased it.

It was a big deal to me. Simply setting a date for that jogging milestone triggered a sense of achievement. I decided I would write an article drawing parallels between my disruption and the unseen difficulties people face around us all the time. I felt that the COVID-19 pandemic meant many people were navigating a heightened level of uncertainty.

The article was titled 'Value Every Step'. It was the first time I had put anything on social media about my 15-month battle. I had simply never seen it as an effective use of my energy and felt publicising my efforts was more likely to distract me than assist me.

The process of writing 'Value Every Step' caused me to address many of the demons that were still haunting me. I knew that I had taken a series of notes on my iPad over my 52 days in hospital, but I could never face opening those notes to read them. I felt uncomfortable about immersing myself in the feelings I experienced during those first few weeks. I didn't feel strong enough yet to relive the uncertainty, the fear, the despair, and I knew those emotions were deeply attached to the events I had recorded.

I forced myself to read those notes, and to play the video of my first attempt to walk from day ten in hospital. My only previous attempt to watch that footage had been in October 2019, and I had turned away in tears. The footage triggered intense feelings of identity loss and shame. It took several attempts, but as I wrote about my challenges, I became more capable of watching my first steps.

'Value Every Step' led to a lot of positive encouragement and rekindled connections that had become barely embers. I received broad encouragement to write and speak further, and the most influential of these gentle interventions was from Kirsten.

Kirsten and I met in early 2017 after I was made redundant. She was assigned as my outplacement support for a few months. We had a slightly rocky start which I think helped shape a mutual appreciation. We kept in contact every six to nine months or so, just a quick email update. When she saw my LinkedIn post, she reached out by telephone and shared how powerful she felt my story was, and how strongly she believed I needed to share my learnings. The call went for a while. It cascaded into that precious time when she was collecting her children from school. When she would normally be enjoying their news, she was investing in me. Encouraging me to borrow her belief – just like Lucy, Clare, Brian, Steely and so many others had done in those first hours and days.

It took me a few months to process, to feel comfortable with her feedback and endorsement. In that interim I was thinking about it often: was she right? If I put my story out there, would people genuinely find it interesting? I couldn't see how it would contribute meaningfully when there are so many inspiring stories to read or hear. I was concerned about stepping into the uncertainty, but mostly I was sceptical about the payback. I could put a lot of effort in and fail. I struggled to believe.

I put my story onto a set of PowerPoint slides. I shared it with a few people, but I couldn't present the slides without breaking down.

I was struggling to visualise how I could find any success from sharing my story.

Then Brian popped up again. He dropped by our house and humbled me. He asked me to share my story with his AFL team: a short talk about navigating adversity. This was the 'Stronger with Them' speech that I referenced in chapter 10.

I was nervous, I was emotional, I was raw. And while I got some really uplifting feedback, I was focusing on the shortfalls in how I spoke versus my aspiration. I felt anxious as I started playing back the video that had recorded my speech – I would have preferred to not watch it at all, but I knew I had to if I was going to learn and improve. As I was telling this to a friend, Justin, he challenged and dissolved my self-deprecation with two simple questions:

1. When you look at that video, what do you see?
2. What would you say to me if it was me talking there?

Justin caused me to acknowledge how much fear and uncertainty I still carried about my future. By exposing how much more generously I would be critiquing him, Justin shifted my focus from the imperfections towards the positives. It was another small intervention moving me towards becoming a fraction stronger.

I committed to facing my fear. I decided to write and trial a keynote speech, and to write this book. In doing so I knew I could readily fail, that both might fall flat with their intended audiences. But my sense of gratitude was driving me to share, and the positive feedback I was getting as I developed and refined my material was providing me with a reinvigorated sense of meaning.

There were just so many moments like these that built off each other. No huge force, just a series of small acts that led to me becoming a fraction stronger. Stepping into uncertainty again to liberate possibility. Investing effort into a new chapter of my life story.

A chapter that is still being written but encourages me that I will like the end.

Before my accident I was living life at a hectic pace. I was upheaved off that treadmill with a crunch. It left me feeling helpless regularly. It rendered me hopeless occasionally. The gentle interventions from so many around me helped me navigate my way back towards self-worth. My own interventions – through rekindling embers, applying effort or reframing my demons – were equally influential.

My future is determined by what I do today. Each day is a new beginning. There is potential in each moment. Where I reach on an emotional and physical recovery level is a function of what I do from now, to sustain and extend my effort and rewards. I know that fraction by fraction I have developed the strength to find myself, no matter what transpires.

There is a Japanese proverb that says, 'The sun does not know good, the sun does not know bad. The sun illuminates and warms everyone equally. Whoever finds himself is like the sun.'

I hope this book has shown you that people can find their worth in many ways. That small efforts applied with consistent conviction, starting from the worst of days, can lead to big outcomes.

I humbly hope a few of my experiences connected with you in some way and created a spark that might help you resolve to set new goals and step into uncertainty towards them. You might even smile and think, 'I was a fraction stronger than I thought', or 'I am now a fraction stronger. I can do more than I ever believed.' I'd love that spirit.

Or perhaps a certain reflection will just rest with you – reside in you as an ember, ready to be rekindled in your moment of need. Just like memories of Karni Liddell and Alan Marshall did for me.

I'd like that a lot.

'It matters not how strait the gate,
How charged with punishments the scroll,
I am the master of my fate,
I am the captain of my soul.'

– William Ernest Henley (Invictus)

Gratitude

To Lucy, Luke, Imogen and Charlie for their acceptance, love and wisdom.

To my parents, for fostering my curiosity and determination while providing the opportunities that put me on a pathway to being a fraction stronger.

To my family, friends and our network, without whom I never could have navigated my recovery as successfully. Your visits, calls, advice, kindness, encouragement and praise were priceless.

To Brooke Lyons, who is simply the best ally, editor and inspiration anyone could possibly hope for. Without you on my team both this project and my sense of worth would be fractions weaker.

To Jacqueline Nagle, Kelly Irving and Lesley Williams for their faith. By provoking me to pursue a fraction more on many levels, you elevated this book to what it is today.

To the Major Street Publishing team for their guidance in helping this book reach its potential.

To Tess McCabe for her brilliant cover design, and the way that makes me feel whenever I see it.

To my writing buddies Bron, Ian and Scotty, for your moral support and encouragement.

To Brian for the essential belief and gentle interventions.

To Kirsten for that Friday afternoon call.

To Alan and Mark for their mentorship over decades and their crucial support at various points of my journey to finding worth.

To Miranda, Karen, Fiona and all the team at Restore Function Physiotherapy. I simply would not be as strong or capable without your care and expertise.

To Dr Carol, the most compassionate and thorough GP a family could wish for.

To the two paramedics who provided the crucial first point of care.

To my surgeons: Andrew (rods in) and Dennis (rods out). I am a testament to your skill.

To the many, many medical professionals including at RBWH Acute Care (Ward 7A Orthopaedics), PAH GARU, GPH and Groove Health. There are way too many – and my memory is too poor to list – but I must at least mention Andy, Adriana, Carolina, Christine, Finn, Jacqui, Leanne, Lucy W, Madi, Mark, Margi, Nick, Nicole, Pia, Scott, Tammy, Teresa, Tracy and Trish.

To the National Disability Insurance Scheme for its important support.

To the many other people who positively influenced my recovery that I could have added: thank you.

You collectively created the constellation of support that made this possible.

About the author

Mark Berridge is a father of three exceptional children and the loving husband of Lucy.

Mark's international corporate career came to an abrupt halt in March 2019 when he fractured two vertebrae and five bones in a bicycling accident. A severe spinal cord injury triggered a personal battle to overcome the ongoing muscular and sensory impacts of his accident.

Mark's determination to achieve an exceptional recovery was driven by the intense fear of those first hours, weeks and days; by his sudden and deep sense of a fractured identity – an identity he desperately wanted back.

Mark now writes and speaks about facing adversity, and the actions and attitudes that supported his recovery. His joy for life, curiosity, personal empathy and hunger for improvement provide the foundation of his work. He is passionate about motivating people to pursue better outcomes and find their worth in life.

Mark is no stranger to disruption and change, having worked in sales, marketing, negotiation, logistics, strategy and business transformation. He has more than 25 years' corporate experience, principally at Rio Tinto, where his pinnacle role was the Chief Negotiator for Rio Tinto Iron Ore as the price custodian of more than US$20 billion in annual revenue.

Mark provides consulting services through his company Refreshing Value and is currently a Senior Associate at Negotiation Partners.

Mark and family are passionate Brisbane Lions supporters who enjoy art, music, travel and nature. Mark is happiest with sand between his toes and the sound of waves in his ears.

www.markberridge.com.au

References

Chapter 1 – Finding your brave face

Margaret M. Perlis 2013, '5 characteristics of grit – how many do you have?' *Forbes*, forbes.com/sites/margaretperlis/2013/10/29/5-characteristics-of-grit-what-it-is-why-you-need-it-and-do-you-have-it/?sh=6a3049504f7b.

Chapter 2 – Embracing uncertainty

Jim Collins & William Lazier 2020, *Beyond Entrepreneurship 2.0: Turning Your Business Into an Enduring Great Company*, Penguin.

Archy O de Berker et. al. 2016, 'Computations of uncertainty mediate acute stress responses in humans', *Nature Communications*, vol. 7.

Danielle Einstein 2015, 'Life is full of uncertainty, we've just got to learn to live with it', The Conversation, theconversation.com/life-is-full-of-uncertainty-weve-just-got-to-learn-to-live-with-it-30092.

Richard Plenty & Terri Morrissey 2020, *Uncertainty Rules? Making uncertainty work for you*, Cork University Press.

Kate Morgan 2020, 'How to function in times of uncertainty', BBC Worklife, bbc.com/worklife/article/20201104-how-to-function-in-times-of-uncertainty.

Elisabeth Kübler-Ross 1969, *On Death and Dying*, Scribner.

Chapter 3 – Liberating possibility

Paul Scott [executive producer] 2013–2015, *Redesign My Brain* [television program], ABC Television.

Sharon Begley 2007, 'The brain: how the brain rewires itself', *TIME*, http://content.time.com/time/magazine/article/0,9171,1580438,00.html.

Bangert, Marc & Eckart O Altenmüller 2003, 'Mapping perception to action in piano practice: a longitudinal DC-EEG study', *BMC Neuroscience* 4: 26.

Cara Feinberg 2010, 'The mindfulness chronicles', *Harvard Magazine*, https://www.harvardmagazine.com/2010/09/the-mindfulness-chronicles.

Tom McDonald 2010, 'The young ones: can re-living your youth make you young again?', BBC TV blog, https://www.bbc.co.uk/blogs/tv/2010/09/the-young-ones.shtml.

BBC News 2010, 'Can you trick your ageing body into feeling younger?', https://www.bbc.com/news/magazine-11284180.

Chapter 10 – Reframing guilt

Francis J. Flynn 2011, 'Defend your research: guilt-ridden people make great leaders', *Harvard Business Review*, https://hbr.org/2011/01/defend-your-research-guilt-ridden-people-make-great-leaders.

Patrick J. Kiger 2018, 'Feeling guilty? That could be a good thing', Stanford Graduate School of Business, https://www.gsb.stanford.edu/insights/feeling-guilty-could-be-good-thing.

Chapter 11 – Facing fear

Greater Good Science Center 2016, 'Overcoming a fear', Greater Good in Action, ggia.berkeley.edu/practice/overcoming_a_fear.

Even better live

My favourite band is Weddings Parties Anything, and many of my important embers relate to Weddings memories that I treasure: listening to their songs with friends; singing along at their epic performances or as I drove my little yellow Corolla around the wide open country roads of Western Australia. After years of encouragement, in 1999 Weddings finally released a live album, aptly called They Were Better Live. I think that applies to us all – we are better live!

A Fraction Stronger captures the spirit of how I tackled my challenges, and how important our conversations and thoughts can be on such a journey. But I know the discussions we share, and the impact I can have, are even better live.

To engage further, find out more via **www.markberridge.com. au** reach out to connect@markberridge.com.au or follow me at **www. linkedin.com/in/mark-berridge**.

Be better with business books

MAJOR STREET

We hope you enjoy reading this book. We'd love you to post a review on social media or your favourite bookseller site. Please include the hashtag #majorstreetpublishing.

Major Street Publishing specialises in business, leadership, personal finance and motivational non-fiction books. If you'd like to receive regular updates about new Major Street books, email info@majorstreet.com.au and ask to be added to our mailing list.

Visit majorstreet.com.au to find out more about our books (print, audio and ebooks) and authors, read reviews and find links to our Your Next Read podcast.

We'd love you to follow us on social media.

- linkedin.com/company/major-street-publishing
- facebook.com/MajorStreetPublishing
- instagram.com/majorstreetpublishing
- @MajorStreetPub